American Realism Revisited

American Realism Revisited

✦

Lethal Minds & Latent Threats

Hakim J Hazim

iUniverse, Inc.
New York Lincoln Shanghai

American Realism Revisited
Lethal Minds & Latent Threats

iUniverse books may be ordered through booksellers or by contacting:

iUniverse
2021 Pine Lake Road, Suite 100
Lincoln, NE 68512
www.iuniverse.com
1-800-Authors (1-800-288-4677)

ISBN-13: 978-0-595-37033-7 (pbk)
ISBN-13: 978-0-595-81436-7 (ebk)
ISBN-10: 0-595-37033-0 (pbk)
ISBN-10: 0-595-81436-0 (ebk)

Printed in the United States of America

THE AUTHOR DEDICATES THIS BOOK

To patriots of every age who fearlessly fought for the dream of such a country long ago

To those who have made it a reality by standing on the shoulders of those before them

To those who labor in order to correct her past and present injustices

To those who dream still, of better days ahead

Contents

Acknowledgements

I want to acknowledge Christ Jesus, my savior.

I want to thank my parents who instilled in me the values of hard work, perseverance and conviction. They are the embodiment of honor and sacrificial living.

I want to thank my siblings, all seven of them, who have all managed to design a life of purpose and meaning, inspiring me in more ways and on more levels than I can number.

I want to thank my lovely wife who has continually supported my efforts. You will always be the gentle breeze that refreshes my day, my zephyr.

I also thank the educators, elders, religious leaders, philosophers, ministers and people of diverse faiths who have taught me to appreciate the pursuit of knowledge.

Introduction

This is a book about ideas, ideas that have been translated into action. It is arranged in the chronological order my papers were written, dating from the days of graduate school to my current research on Iraq. The ideas espoused by individuals, groups, and nations form worldviews and ideologies. They motivate, justify, galvanize and lead to particular destinations. I have studied the major ideas that have manifested into political and religious movements during the course of world history. Two primary ideas have been of interest to the US since the end of WWII: communism and idea based terrorism. Communism was paramount in the minds of American statesmen before its collapse, and now the counterfeit form of Islam has led the US to wage war against another ideology. My interest in these two subjects led to enrollment at Cal State University San Bernardino, where I studied these and graduated from the national security studies program. Themes of freedom, oppression and deliverance are often used as war cries for change and revolution. These themes are resident in the minds of statesmen and individuals when they act. It is time to examine the ideas and efforts of statesmen currently engaged in promoting new or refurbished ideas within their countries or abroad in order to organize people around a philosophy they hope will prevail. It is also time to gain insight into the lethal minds and militant cults that are causing death and destruction while feeding fear and paranoia worldwide. Some of these ideas are religious and others are secular. The world is established upon such ideas, and wars are fought when they collide; the collisions are unavoidable. History proves that war is, unfortunately, a permanent feature in mankind's interactions; lasting ideas have a logical, organizational end.

Seven levels of ideas (The authors philosophical construct):

1. Ideas are birthed and accepted as plausible or rejected.

2. If accepted they are placed into philosophical constructs.

3. Powerful individuals or groups migrate towards these ideas and create momentum or movements.

4. Conflicting ideas between groups lead to conflict or compromise. In some cases, the ideas are incorporated into an already existing philosophy and at other times, during an impasse, the conflict may become physical in nature, resulting in war.

5. The emerging winner bases the group or nation on the idea or philosophy.

6. Laws will be passed reflecting these ideas.

7. The state or group enforces these laws.

When ideas collide in the form of warfare, an approach to warfare must be formulated. If war is a historical axiom, then there must be an approach to warfare that the majority of statesmen in the world have accepted. There has primarily been one dominant school of thought in political science concerning warfare since WWII, Realism. Reinhold Neibuhr, a Protestant theologian, is credited as having a profound effect on the moral philosophy of warfare by most political scientists, and he had a direct effect on the founder of realism as a theory, Hans Morganthau. The term and theory realism was articulated by Morgenthau who paid homage to Niebuhr on several occasions. [1] The latter more technical term, neorealism, introduced by Ken Waltz revived interest in the theory, interest that continues in practice by statesmen to this day. Realism has served statesmen and scholars as both an explanatory tool and way of dealing with national and international threats. Terms such as balance of power, zero-sum, bandwagoning, security dilemma, and strategic balance have entered into our modern vocabulary.

Let me state for the record that I am a realist and have been influence by all three men mentioned above, primarily Niebuhr. I believe that history tells us that large, organized groups of people, whether villages, clans, city-states or the modern nation states, are the primary driving forces in politics and warfare. These groups will ultimately succeed or fail. Failure means they are conquered or simply implode into chaos; at times implosion occurs because of the influence of foreign nations; failing states remain problematic. The real struggle that lies ahead for nations in this category is to provide for the basic needs of their people in terms of economics and politics. Realism is an idea or theory that claims to show nations how to maintain their sovereignty when conflict arises. Dominant ideologies that govern nations in the international community have been placed there by powerful nations. This was proven by the polarity between communism and democracy during the Cold War. The ideas that nations are based on will pass away if countries are not able to maintain sovereignty and fall prey to aggressive nations; the idea, like the nation, may perish.

Somewhere in the discourse of foreign policy, there is a taboo subject that few speak of in this era of superpower coziness; it is the proverbial elephant in the room. I'm speaking of hostile states that may be willing to either fight unconventionally through sponsoring terrorism or strike the US first with nuclear weapons in warfare. I simplify it further by calling this category, *latent threats*. The latent threats include, but are not limited to the following states: China, Iran, North Korea and a resurgent Russia. Russia is still a present threat to the US and marshals a formidable nuclear arsenal that should cause policy analysts great concern. The deteriorating situation with Chechens and foreign fighters has certainly caused this nation to look inward, but that does not in any way deter it from its historical pattern of aggression. Russia is still one of the gravest threats to American security and will be heavily addressed in the second section of this book.

Author's personal view

I am not a Muslim; I am a former Muslim. My take on terrorism combines personal experience and scholarly objectivity. My personal experience draws from two religious backgrounds, my adult faith, Christianity, and my childhood faith of Black Nationalism and self-sufficiency taught early on by the Nation of Islam until it merged with the non-race based approach of orthodox Sunnism after the death of Elijah Muhammad. I find myself fielding questions all of the time because of my name. Many are surprised to know that I am a believer in Christ as savior. Ultimately what qualifies me to undertake this task are the following credentials: my experience with the faith, degrees: BA in Sociology and MA in National Security, experience as an educator, consultant work with law enforcement agencies, the military, and my past experience as a correctional officer.

It should be noted that the orthodox faith of Islam poses no militant threat to society at large, and people of faith and all fair-minded individuals should be able to recognize all of the vile forms of religion that seek to offer spiritual guidance as a means of carrying out the sadistic intentions of some narcissistic individuals who are deluded in their understanding of faith. But it is clear that terrorists invoke religion and use it in order to recruit. Muslims may hate this reality, but it does not change the fact that terrorists call themselves true believers and are growing exponentially. The true and the counterfeit must be distinguished. This cannot be done without examining their doctrine. I define Al Qaeda as a militant cult, not Muslims; it is a counterfeit movement.

Since September 11 the international community has been saturated by a myriad of books and articles on the subject of terrorism, mistakenly labeling it

Islamic Terrorism. The author has decided to write yet another one. It is my hope that this attempt will not be an ostentatious explanation of what is taking place currently or worse yet an oversimplification of the phenomenon known as terrorism. It is my fervent desire to shed light through this series of papers. Before and during my undergraduate training I began studying terrorism within militia groups and regional jihads. My graduate training in security studies led me to believe early on that terrorism would indeed become a significant national security issue and threat. "Middle Eastern Interpretations of Jihad and the Far-reaching Consequences", written in May 2001, was my first attempt to write a scholarly paper on the subject. This was followed up that summer by my second research document presented to the National Law Enforcement and Technology Center that downloaded and analyzed several doctrines on the Internet that were calling for a jihad against the US. The document was named "Foreign OPFOR Reader: Radical Islamic and Al Qaeda Doctrine." Things were heating up then, and those familiar with this research had a gut feeling something was about to happen. I have critics that say I am an apologist for Muslims; others state I am against Muslims, and others question my motivations on a range of issues. I'll never satisfy the critics and will not address them formally in this book. I'll simply challenge them to give the research an honest look.

After September 11 hit, the international community was forever changed. The myth of state actors alone possessing the power to wage war was shattered, and all of our notions of invincibility vanished. Unfortunately there were warnings not heeded by heads of states, and the ideology and worldviews behind terrorism continued to spread throughout the Middle East, Central Asia, Eastern Europe, Western Europe, America, Africa and other regions as well. The virus was nurtured and funded by nations such as Saudi Arabia and Pakistan. The Mujihadeen who once served as an extension of state policy sought their own nation and turned their backs on those who nurtured them, giving rise to treacherous offspring that would return to haunt the countries of America, Saudi Arabia and Pakistan. They declared war, on all infidels, crusaders and apostates.

Terrorism has changed the face of America, even her soul. A few more attacks, and we will become more and more like a police state. Democracy as we once knew it is forever changed, and we may be playing a dirge for it as it once existed with the privileges of freedom and privacy in the coming years, probably out of necessity. There is no shortage of militant cults, and unfortunately those who are willing to follow them. Last of all, I've enclosed a poem that is a challenge to people questioning what they hear from their leaders. Keep in mind, some ideas are simple to understand but very dangerous. I have compassion for people who find themselves under the sway of a false leader steering them towards their own destruction. I write this with them in mind.

A Seer

You don't need a seer to take your hand and lead you in the way.
No thundering prophets to arouse your fear of the day.
Your heart is filled with nobility and sins that entice.
Yet it contains a conscience offering sound advice.
It guides, restrains and recognizes wisdom from diverse voices.
It distinguishes between prophets and moral choices.
Believe that you have a compass.
God has not left us alone.
Trust this.

Endnote

1. Landon, Harold, Reinhold Niebuhr A Prophetic Voice in Our Time (Greenwich; The Seabury Press, 1962) p. 109

Realism Revisited: Dual Challenges of Terrorism and Latent Threats

By H. Hazim

November 2001

Excerpt From

HISTORY OF THE PELOPONNESIAN WAR
431 BC by Thucydides

CHAPTER XVII.
Sixteenth Year of the War—The Melian Conference—Fate of Melos

Melians. But we know that the fortune of war is sometimes more impartial than the disproportion of numbers might lead one to suppose; to submit is to give ourselves over to despair, while action still preserves for us a hope that we may stand erect.
Athenians. *Hope, danger's comforter, may be indulged in by those who have abundant resources, if not without loss at all events without ruin; but its nature is to be extravagant, and those who go so far as to put their all upon the venture see it in its true colors only when they are ruined; but so long as the discovery would enable them to guard against it, it is never found wanting. Let not this be the case with you, who are weak and hang on a single turn of the scale; nor be like the vulgar, who, abandoning such security as human means may still afford, when visible hopes fail them in extremity, turn to invisible, to prophecies and oracles, and other such inventions that delude men with hopes to their destruction.*

Basic Tenets of Realism

1. The international community is basically anarchic and without any permanent law enforcer.
2. Nations are driven by self-interest and seek to maintain autonomy in their internal affairs and increase their power and influence abroad.
3. The state/nation is the primary actor in the international community, and powerful nations direct the course of the international system.
4. Nations sometimes choose to settle their scores through going to war when they deem it necessary.
5. Power is the key in this theory; nations that possess economic and military power are able to glean most of the benefits from the international system.
6. Nations measure themselves in terms of power, primarily militarily and economically.
7. Weaker nations form alliances and coalitions as a way of balancing and dealing with more powerful nations.
(Synopsis was gleaned from the research of Reinhold Neigbuhr, Hans Morgenthau and Kenneth Waltz.)

America is fighting a weaker enemy, who has smaller numbers and is driven by religious delusions and ideas. Latent threats in the form of nations are what America has always trained for. Latent threats are nations that are not engaged in warfare against America but clearly remain a threat to US security. Buoyed by recent terrorist attacks, jihad enthusiasts are continuing a supranational campaign against America and the West itself, giving rise to non-state threats that target the American way of life. This is frightening, but America must weigh it threats and not lose sight of the danger of our latent threats, traditional enemies in the form of nations. The author of this paper is a realist, so the approach toward politics is state-centric, meaning powerful nations/states decide the fate of the international community. The paper is limited to discussing realism in terms of the state as the primary actor in international relations. Further, it is undertaken due to the recent attacks on American soil that changed previous assumptions concerning terrorist's capabilities. America's enemies are no longer state-centric alone, and they are capable of wreaking havoc on American soil. However, national security is concerned with defending state sovereignty and protecting its citizens domestically. With this in mind, terrorism must be approached from a state-centric perspective in spite of burgeoning non-state threats.

Although Al Qaeda's stated goal is expansionist and supranational; it still has political motivations. This militant cult is bound to the allegiance of a distorted caliph type (Usamah bin Laden) who seeks to lead them in a campaign to reshape the world into its version of the Garden of God one nation at a time.[1] The major concern of the Bush Administration is this is a new type of warfare that does not owe its allegiance to a state and seeks to overcome the very structure of every state that does not adhere to its worldview. Martin vanCreveld has written a great deal about the changing pattern of conflict and the decline of the state.[2] He and others believe that terrorism and other types of low intensity conflict will become the greatest threat to civilization's future. However, the disturbing assertion that terrorism (and other forms of low-intensity conflict) may be the greatest threat to states and civilization in general is not credible in light of the countless millions of lives that state sponsored wars have cost humanity. Although new emerging threats of international terrorism will prove challenging for our military and intelligence branches, they lack the arsenals and political organization of state actors and cannot be considered the primary threat to national security.

The weapons and politics employed in previous and current wars by powerful states were, and still remain, unequaled by any non-state actor, and this is precisely why terrorists covet the weapons and political sophistication of modern states. Whether these weapons are conventional, biological, psychological or nuclear, states have a monopoly on the majority of them, especially the more powerful ones.[3] Who can forget the appeal to nationalism by Hitler and the consequences that followed his politics? As far as politics, if Carl Von Clausewitz was correct and war is fought for a political end, then the logical end of a terrorist's strategy would be violence as an extension of policy, similar to a state, but bolder and less civilized. States are constrained by international opinion and the sentiments of their members. The people, political leaders, and military leadership must be unified in order for war to be effectively sustained. However, if there is great division, problems began to emerge, and the Clausewitzian trinity breaks down. [4] Terrorists seek to convert people to their ideas before they ever attempt to train them for warfare. Warfare is a political action taken to the level of violence and once waged all three sides of a nation's participants must remain in balance and harmony in order to have continued success. The diagram below illustrates this.

Political Leaders

People   Military

When a state makes war against another state or a domestic enemy, part of its success lies in its ability to control and guide its members by certain ideas. These ideas build upon other ideas that have come before them. Great nations have had ideological glue behind its politics that solidified consensus, moved its people forward and conquered their foes and eventually formed allies with other nations, exporting their ideas in the process. The state must always look for ways to create a favorable consensus among the newly conquered population or subjects towards their new leadership after war is over. A cursory look at Western history over the last eight hundred years will show the progressive movements that formed modern democracy. One feature of modern democracy is that dissent within often leads to new movements of reform and at times revolution and war. Britain limited the power of the king with the Magna Carta nearly eight centuries ago, and this increased the nobles' voice and rights within the kingdom. A few centuries later, Martin Luther broke the strangle hold of religious tyranny in Germany from the common man's neck, laying the foundation for industrialization and each man's work having value; this was movement was named Protestantism. Later, British settlers in America shook off the weight of England's perceived tyranny and formed the world's first great democracy. This slowly began to emerge into a new way of governing and the evidence of this was manifested in America's ability to convince conquered foes who were also industrialized nations such as Japan and Germany that democracy's free way of life is the best form of government.

Terrorists, as of the present, lack the idea capital to convert a large majority of people to their cause or significant numbers of Muslims away from orthodox Islam; therefore, few have joined their declaration of war. (Although the small number who have are causing havoc.) The political sophistication of their philosophy is simplistic and sufficient for their small numbers, but the greater the numbers, the more potential for division and problems. This is one reason that terrorists have not historically worked together, but that may be changing as the gharb's influence stretches into their world and creates more Western animosity.[5]

The idea capital is severely lacking in countries that terrorists tend to emerge from, giving rise to a general dissatisfaction of the people, and even worse, terrorism. The dissatisfaction of the populations of Third-world countries is understandable in light of the fact that they have never been through a period of enlightenment or significant modernization and remain in perpetual poverty. While the majority of the world is bent on consumerism and material acquisition, the ideological culture of terrorists cause them to seek ways of overthrowing the Western way of life and the ruling statesmen partial to it within their nations. By seeking to advance Western influence into Islamic lands that do not agree with its approach, America may be creating a serious problem.

Failing states are a natural part of the international system and dissatisfaction mounts within them. Groups that desire recognition as a state, such as the PLO and Tamil organization fall into this category. At this point myths are created and people are instructed to look for a state in the afterlife and have their security needs met there. It's effective. A new state in paradise where God himself is the just ruler is one perk for the religious; for secular groups one achieves immortality through memory of his great deed and the cult of martyrdom formed. These are the desired ends of suicide bombers, and this appears rational to them and when one considers this and the security needs of any group, it becomes evident that this type of desperation grows out of the dissatisfaction that terrorists have within their own nations. [6] The idea of a state is just as valuable to terrorists as it is to anyone else. The state system is built upon the foundation of Clausewitz. Al Qaeda has stated on numerous occasions that it seeks to overthrow apostate regimes and replace these leaders with their own. Palestinian terrorism has successfully implemented the Clausewitz triangle by unifying the people, military leadership, and political leadership around the singular idea of Palestinian statehood, and the justification of terrorism as a means to that end.

When terrorism is viewed as a political action, state centric models begin to make sense. Dr. Mark T. Clark asks two relevant questions in his essay, "The Continuing Relevance of Clausewitz" and the questions were these: What are non-state actors after, and is Clausewitz's model of the trinity still relevant when dealing with these groups? Terrorists clearly have a political agenda, but do they have the genius (military leadership) and the passion (people behind them)? The balance of all three sides of the triangle must remain in sync. Clark suggests that further research must be done in this area if theorists are going to come to any meaningful conclusions about the role of non-state actors in warfare. He argues, persuasively, that these non-state actors are still using Clausewitz's trinity in their approach to warfare. Clearly there is a great deal of evidence that war is a political end, and people want to be sovereign and direct their own affairs without outside influence. This desire for autonomy is manifested throughout history. [7] States do desire a particular end and will do whatever it takes to protect their interests and even more when their sovereignty is threatened. In this sense, terrorists are the same as states and owe their loyalty to a group, even if it is transnational. It provides them with the things their current nations cannot. Consider these individuals to be in a state of transition until a new state emerges.

The technological limitations of terrorists are evident as well. By using primitive delivery systems to attack (suicide bombers, mail, trucks, cars and airplanes) they reveal a glaring weakness in technological capability when compared with states. By contrasting this with the history of states, a pattern will begin to emerge. Dr.Robert Bunker and Dr. Martin vanCreveld rightly assert that technology has been the key instrument in the development of any great nation or state. From the Roman gladius to match-lit aquebus, technologically advanced societies were always able to force other less developed societies to succumb to their wills. This factor alone explains why some nations have had aspirations to become great military powers but lacked the capability to achieve it. Other nations may boast of a great army and unlimited manpower, but they lacked the technological tools and sophistication to sustain any type of revolt. The British are one example; they routinely dominated nations that outnumbered them due to their mastery of the seas and superior land arsenals. [8]

As a state responds to terrorism, the obvious begins to emerge; terrorism cannot exist without state support or tolerance.

Attacking terrorism will involve dealing with other states, as recently demonstrated by the US invasion of Afghanistan. These cells exist in states and must be restrained by states. The complicated and inexplicable relationship between states and terrorists can be seen within the government of Afghanistan. Afghanistan was the only country that would openly support bin Laden. As calls for greater interdependence on the part of the nations of the world to fight this growing threat go out, other cells will pay a similar price. America's plans must take into account multi-national political constraints, because the inverse relationship between multilateral and unilateral action cannot be reconciled. There must be a great deal of caution taken so other Islamic states (nations containing large Muslim populations) are not offended, and calls for jihad are not legitimately sent out. States that are latent threats may be considering state sponsored terrorism against the US and this should remain as a primary concern. To imply otherwise, one must assume that human nature has miraculously changed, and our old enemies have not taken some pleasure in the recent terrorist attacks against America. If there is a willingness to cooperate, it is born out of the knowledge that these organizations pose a significant threat to all nations. The terrorism threat is not as great as that of a state actor becoming active against America, due to the fact they have not acquired the weaponry or delivery systems they desire. [9]

Terrorists have previously succeeded in carrying out attacks against America. Two accounts of this were the two attacks on the World Trade Center in February of 93 and September 11, 2001. Both attacks took sophistication in planning but used primitive delivery systems. Although three of the attacks achieved their targets, one failed to. The 1993 incident also achieved moderate success, but failed to achieve its ultimate objective, greater lethality. The Tokyo Sarin Nerve Gas Attack in Japan followed this, and this proved to be a well thought out attack, but it failed to produce the degree of carnage the cult intended. This attack was motivated by domestic terrorists but is included here to show the lack of effectiveness of terrorists when compared with the sophistication of state machinery. [10] These attacks brought terrorism into full view. The greatest domestic attack in US history was the Oklahoma City bombing. Oklahoma City proved to be a turning point in the history of terrorism, and the FBI considered the weapon of McVeigh a WMD. [11] From this moment on, terrorists were considered to be a formidable threat to U.S. security, rightfully so, but not to the extent of other nations. Hit and run or suicide operation techniques are common with Terrorism as well as other guerilla warfare tactics.

The limits of terrorists are evidenced further by their inability to mobilize in the open and wage war in a manner that is sustained and consistent. They may in fact attack their targets and attempt to play on the fears of the population, but they are unable to wage war in a way that can effectively break down the will of the enemy. They are limited to an asymmetrical type of warfare that is waged in the shadows and in secret. The goals of such warfare are political and ideological in nature. The techniques that are used are based on the limited technology that they have acquired. The arsenals at their disposal vary, but historically they have failed to show the capacity to cause serious damage to the state infrastructure when compared to the massive casualties inflicted by state actors.

America is at war now, and one point needs to be stressed, historically other countries have joined wars when they saw an opportunity or felt compelled, either overtly or covertly. Recent examples of these were the Vietnam War when the Soviet Union undermined U.S. efforts in Vietnam and the payback of the U.S. in Afghanistan. Secondly, other nations may already be involved and planning an attack if our military shifts its focus in the wrong direction, terrorism only. Terrorism could be a timely diversion for enemies who are waiting for an opportunity to strike at U. S. vulnerability. And lastly, since the world is anarchic and power has always decided the direction and values that would be reflected in international politics, the US must act, because if it fails to show unilateral will and overly relies on coalitions, it will neglect its unique place in history as a unipolar superpower and set a precedent that tells the world that it is reluctant and unwilling to act alone when pursuing enemies. [12]

The state must come up with solutions to deal with transnational actors. The state can wage war on these actors and in doing so inflict great damage to their infrastructure and economic capability. If it does, terrorists will be forced to flee to other states and seek refuge there. Usamah bin Laden has lived in several states since his exile from Saudi Arabia and will undoubtedly be seeking a new home shortly, if he has not already. International terrorism does have a global reach, and the political and military balancing act employed by the Bush administration is less focused on terrorist organizations and more focused on the nations that sponsor them. Indeed, such nations will be easier to deal with directly than the terrorists. Donald Rumsfield recently articulated this in a "U.S.A. Today" interview on the 26th of October 2002. He spoke candidly about the difficulty of capturing bin Laden and stated that, "He may get away." From the freezing of bank accounts, to the pressure placed on state sponsors, and the humanitarian efforts recently undertaken in Afghanistan, America is balancing its interests. This balancing is necessary because of the states involved and the limits of terrorism without state cooperation. [13]

The Bush Administration entered the war against terrorism with a cautious approach because of the nature of militant movements posing as Muslims. Care must be taken in order to distinguish the true from the counterfeit. The name of the first operational title was "Operation Infinite Justice." This title was soon changed upon the revelation that it offended the vast majority of Islamic clerics who stated that only God alone is able to offer such justice. This demonstrated that the administration wanted to do everything in its power to keep from offending Islamic clergy and the masses of Islamic people who lack a great degree of loyalty to their state. Consequently, some could be induced to join the fray of militants. These states must be able to satisfy their populations, or they will give rise to domestic disturbances, uprisings and perhaps civil war. With this in mind, the U.S. must walk a fine line so that fragile coalitions with fragile third world countries prone to coups will not disintegrate. Domestic terrorists have ample time to develop their attacks against the state when they claim they are trying to return to the early generations of the pious. When this message catches on one must ask the question of what is the appropriate response to this especially since movements condoning violent means to an end exist with those who simply want to return to Islamic origins.[14] The Taliban claim this but they are nothing more than a militant cult that came into possession of a state.

The Taliban are a fundamentalist nationalist movement that began as a popularly supported drive to disarm warlords and bring peace to Afghanistan. It has evolved into a Pashtu-dominated force conducting ethnic warfare against the Uzbeks, Tajiks, and Hazara. It is also an oppressive domestic force imposing its own peculiar interpretation of Islamic law on the populace. Hypocritically, they continue to implement methods of warfare prohibited by law upon the Northern Alliance and its population. Torture, rape, drug inducement, chemicals and poisons are all used in their warfare. The Taliban are not a traditional government, tied to buildings, ministries and the conventional infrastructure of a state. Rather, it is a loosely organized confederation of forces, tribal leaders and religious leaders that take its general guidance from Mullah Omar in Kandahar. Together they violate Shariah law and fail to rule effectively and coherently. [15] Omar's edicts are often a function of the local warlords' concerns and his own interests. Consequently, it will be very difficult to completely remove the Taliban from power or influence, since there is no rigid, formal structure. The Taliban are as much an idea as an entity and their influence extends beyond Afghanistan's borders-particularly into Pakistan.

Realism revisited

Although realism and its offspring, neorealism, cannot account for all of the occurrences in the history of warfare it does give an adequate description of what states do to increase or maintain their power. The actions of states are calculated and weighed in terms of their interests. At a minimum, states will do what it takes to survive, and at a maximum they continue to do whatever they can to increase their power. All states fall into this category, whether weak or strong. When a state is bent on increasing its power and seeks to expands it borders it is sometimes called and expansionist state. [16] When a state is threatened with such an aggressor, it will seek ways to defend itself and even form an alliance with a stronger ally to remain sovereign, even if it will be indebted to another in the long term.

The emerging terrorist threat is an international problem, and Al Qaeda is an expansionist organization. Theorists and politicians concur on this point. As the threat continues to emerge, states will have to make decisions that enable them to deal with terrorists. Because of state sovereignty, states will choose the approach to take with terrorists. The approaches will have similarities in some areas and differences in other, but each approach will be a sovereign approach that cooperates with other states and uses unilateral action or a combination of both. Currently, the United States is using a combination of unilateral and cooperative action to deal with the emerging terrorism threat.

Undoubtedly, there are numerous people who are pushing the fact that terrorism is truly dangerous and requires attention. America seems to be moving in the right direction by calling terrorism an international problem that requires international solutions, but what is troubling here is the fact that the crisis may lead to a neglect of traditional enemies. These are the state actors or latent threats that could harm the US far more than any terrorist threat could. Terrorism could also become state sponsored and used to divert many resources into non-conventional operations. Enemies of America are fully aware that she is ill equipped to carry on a war with state actors and non-state actors simultaneously. [17] This two-faced Janus could emerge from several nations when they realize the tremendous opportunity to hit America with covert state sponsored terrorism with one face, while pledging their support with the other. The US must preserve the historical approach of continuing to prepare for state threats, while adapting for terrorism and low intensity conflict. America will be required to act unilaterally at times, but it must only do so with the support of its public.

Unilateral action may be required as it uncovers new threats. Unilateral action requires the will to go it alone when it serves American interests, and this requires conviction and courage on the part of the foreign policy team. America must protect itself from future attacks by state and non-state actors. And just as the ancient Spartans feared the growing power of Athens and acted to prevent its spreading influence, her enemies have feared her growing influence and power for some time but have been unable to act in a way that would cut her down to size. It is a well-known fact that countries such as China, Russia, Iraq, Iran and North Korea see N.A.T.O. and the U.N. as an extension of U.S. intrusion into global affairs. These countries have waited for some time to bring a multi-polar balance to the international community and have actively tried to counter any move concerning US defense initiatives. [18] As America moves toward ridding the world of terrorism, it should keep one eye on the other states that seek to influence its *balance of interests* in the United Nations.

Conclusion

Three Reasons Terrorist Will Continue to act but Fail to Achieve Their Goals

1) The self-help system inherent within the international system will prove to be too formidable a foe for the supranational organizations of terrorists.

2) Terrorists commit acts that will hinder them from receiving acceptance within the international community and the Islamic Ummah (body of believers).

3) The way a state comes into existence is not as important as the fact that it becomes a state, and this is the stated goal of *some* terrorist organizations. If statehood is achieved, the choice for terrorism will end in some cases.

The self-help system is a system that focuses on how and why states cooperate. The organization of states within the international community allow for a self-help system. It enables states to enter into coalitions with one another and derive some type of benefit form cooperation. One of the reasons that terrorists will not be able to wreak the havoc that a state will is due to the fact they have a difficult time securing cooperation from other states, due to the vilification they endure because of their actions which would give rise to a hostile hostile response other nations will heap on those who sponsor them. [19]

The international system understands that they must rid themselves of the forces of terrorism that seek to destroy them. The state must look to the health of its citizens, and the primary way of doing this is to rank the threats to its existence. Although states can provide some type of law and order for its citizens, it must remain leery of its enemies, and enemies can lie within and without its borders. If a group rises up that is opposed to a particular state and is within the borders of that state, the state will take whatever measures necessary to defend itself and its citizens. The state will act rationally in terms of self-defense against internal threats and external threats in order to maintain its preservation. [20]

The lengths that terrorist are willing to go force them to be isolated from the modern world. They can draw from the desperate, frustrated masses of suicide bombers that have little education and little reason to live, or they can draw from the educated Special Forces crew of September 11 and others like them. The fact that September 11 produced something unique and different, does not mean that America, or its allies, should make terrorism the primary concern in military affairs. It is clear that terrorists have placed their enemies under the Middle Eastern Ban and have little regard for civilian lives. Unfortunately, these acts are something the West should come to expect. [21] Terrorism will impact other nations as well and must be dealt with. America could become prophetic if she has to stand alone for a time period and warn other nations of the coming lawlessness that will ensue if terrorists are not dealt with swiftly. In spite of this, America must remember, menacing latent threats remain in the form of nations, so America must be vigilant because many seek to harm us. War is hell, and it must be waged with the will of the populace behind the political leaders and generals. When the US responds militarily it must keep in mind the 6 tenets of the Wienberger doctrine:

1. **The United States should not commit forces to combat unless the vital national interests of the United States or its allies are involved.**

2. **U.S. troops should only be committed wholeheartedly and with the clear intention of winning. Otherwise, troops should not be committed.**

3. **U.S. combat troops should be committed only with clearly defined political and military objectives and with the capacity to accomplish those objectives.**

4. **The relationship between the objectives and the size and composition of the forces committed should be continually reassessed and adjusted if necessary.**

5. **U.S. troops should not be committed to battle without a "reasonable assurance" of the support of U.S. public opinion and Congress.**

6. **The commitment of U.S. troops should be considered only as a last resort.** [22]

These tenets do not guarantee victory, but they do place restraints on the use of warfare, and restraint is always a good thing for democracies.

Bibliography

Al-Buti, Muhammad Sa'id and Salafi teacher "Why Does One Have to Follow a Madhab" 1995
<http://dialspace.dialpipex.com/masud/Islam/nuh/buti.htm>

Ali, Malana Muhammad, *A Manual of Hadith* (The Ahmadiyya Anjuman Ishaat Islam Lahore, New Garden Town, Lahore-16, Pakistan 1986)

Amin, S.H. "Islamic Law and its Implication for the Modern World." *Muslim Education*

Holy Bible

Bodanski, Yosseph, Bin Laden: The Man Who Declared War on America (Prima Publishing) 1999

Maryland 1987)

Coud, David, S. "US Strategy on Saudi Exile Shifts to 'Speak No Evil'", *The Wall Street Journal,* April 3, 2001

Elbarky, Muhammad Mokbe, "Different Concepts of Jihad and its Relevance to Contemporary Ehrenreich, Barbara Katha Politt, et al. "Fukuyama's Follies" Foreign Affairs, Jan/Feb 1999

Fukayama Francis, "The End of History" *The National Interest*, Summer 1989

Gannon, Kathy, "Bin Laden Calls For Continuing Holy War", The Seatle Times Co.

Gulzar, Ahmad, The Concept of War in Islam: Analysis of the ideological Controversy in Pakistan. (London Francis Pinter, 1987)

The Holy Quran

Husain, Mir Zohair. *Global Islamic Politics* (New York: Harper Collins, 1995)

Ely Karmon, "Th e Role of Intelligence in the Fight Against Terrorism," Conference on, "Intelligience in the 21st century"

Keohane, Robert, O. *Neorealism and its Critics*, (Columbia University Press: New York), 1979

Machiavelli, Nicollo, The Discources of Nicollo Machiavelli. Trans. Leslie J. Walker. 2 Vols. (New Haven: Yale University Press, 1950)

Johanna Mcgeary, "Terror in Africa", Time Magazine Aug. 17, 1998 Vol 152 No. 7

Merari, Ariel, "Attacks on Cvil Aviation: Trends and Lessons" *Lecture at White House Commission-GWU Conference on Aviation Safety in the 21st century* <http://www.gwu.edu/cms/aviation/track ii/merari.html> May, 07, 2001

Mernissi, Fatima, Islam and Democracy: Fear of the Modern World (Reading Mass., 1992)

MIPT, "Countering The Changing Threat of International Terrorism", Dec. 1999 <u>http://www.mipt.org/bremerreport.html</u>

Imam Warrith Deen Muhammad, Interview by Omar Hazim, Topeka Ks. Dec 12 2001

Anthony J. Parel *The Machiavellian Cosmos* (Yale University Press,New Haven and London 1992)

Pipes, Daniel, "Dealing With Middle East Conspiracy Theories," ORBIS, Winter 1992 pp.41–56

Salmi, Ralph, Caesar Adib Ma, George K. Tanham, *Islam and Conflict Resolution* (University Press of America, Inc. 4720 Boston Way, Lanham Maryland 1998)

Sicherman, Harvey, Judaism and the World: The Holy and the Profane (Religion in World Affairs) Orbis, Spring 1998

Slavin, Barbara, "Cheney Criticizes Attacks by Isreal" *USA Today* May 21, 2001

US State Department, Patterns of Global Terrorism: Middle East overview April/May 1996–00,

<http://www.usis.usemb.se/terror/rpt1999/mideast.html

Vicki Sullivan, *Machiavellis Three Romes* (Northern Illinois University Press, DeKalb, Ill. 1996)

Taheri, Amir, *Holy Terror* (Adler & Adler, Publishers Inc. 4550 Montgomery Ave. Bethesda

3875Atherton Rd. Rocklin California, 95765,1999)

Tomsen, Peter "A Chance For Peace in Afghanistan" Foreign Affairs, Jan/FEb 2000

—-Trends of Islamic Movements" The Jerusalem Journal of International Relations 9, Dec.19 1987)

Martin Van Creveld, "The Fate of the State" (Parameters, Spring) 1996 pp. 4–18

Waltz, Kenneth, N., *Man the State and War*, (New York: Columbia University Press) 1959

Waltz, Kenneth, N., *The Theory of International Politics,*(Reading, Mass Addison Wesley) 1979

Bruce Maddy-Weitzman, "The Islamic Challenge in North America" *Meria* vol. 1 No.2 July 1997

Yusufzai, Rahimullah "Conversations With Terror", <u>Time Magazine</u>, Jan. 11, 1999 Vol. 153 No. 1

Footnotes

1.Taheri, Amir, Holy Terror, pp. 19–29
2. Van Creveld, "The Fate of the State

3. Clark, Mark T., [International Relations Theory, Seminar], Fall 2000 "Neorealism"

4. Clausewitz, Carl Von, *On War,* Translated by Grahm, J.J., Edited by Rapaport, Anatol, (Originally published in 1832, This publication is Penguin Groups, LTD 27 Wrights Lane, London, England) pp.116–125

5. Gharb is a territory of the strange, forbidden and dark. The sun sets here and all manner of fearful terrifying activities take place. It is symbolic and has been used to represent the Western world and its influences. (Mernissi, Fatima, Islam and Democracy: Fear of a Modern World. [Secondary source found in Bruce Maddy-Wietzman, Islamic Challenge in North America])

6 Van Creveld, "The Fate of the State"

7. Dr. Clark, "The Continuing Relevance of Clausewitz

8. Bunker, Robert, "Vassal Warfare" Lecture series "Evolution of Warfare"

9. Associated Press

10. US Department of State, *Pattern of Global Terrorism.* 1997,98,99,-00

11. CNN, America Strikes Back, 11/24 01

12. Dr. Clark, Interview.

13. USA Today, October 26, 2002, exclusive with Rumsfield

14. The Salafi are known as the First Three Generations of Islam. These included the Prophet's lifetime and the two following him. The prophet stated that these would be the best and most devoted Muslims. The Salafi Movement is seen by some as a heretical cult. The movement is characterized by a new devotion to the scriptures and Hadiths while emphasizing the teaching of the Quran and Hadiths while wanting to return to the purity of the first three generations. The problems that accompany this movement are the fear of another sect that adheres to a different viewpoint and refuses to acknowledge orthodox authority. The majority of Salafi's are not violent nor do they seek a violent overthrow of the government. Taken From Interview with Dr. Salmi, May, 4, 2001Caliph is a term used for the first four successors of Muhammad. They were (in order): Abu Bakr (632–34), Umar (634–44), Uthman (644–56), Ali (656–61).

15. The acts mentioned above as permissible are taken form the Hadiths and Quran (The Hadith is a book of the prophets sayings or quotes during his life on the earth and it was compiled by trusted scribes and close companions) Although, there are some points of disagreement regarding the use of poison arrows are daggers, the majority of jurists, imams and scholars agree with this list. Taken from Salmi, Majul, Tanham, *Islam and Conflict Resolution* pp.123–30

<http://usinfo.state.gov/cgi-bin...=/products/washfile/newsitem.shtml> May 11, 2001

16. Waltz, International Relations Theory
17. Ibid
18. Ibid
19. Ibid
20. Ibid.
21. Bodanski, Yosseph, Bin Laden : The Man Who Declared War on America. pp.28–83
22. US Secretary of Defense Caspar Weinberger, "The Uses of Military Power" delivered before the National Press Club in Washington, D.C., November 28, 1984

Atta's Letter: Insight into a lethal Mind

Muhammad Atta was the perfect example of a lethal mind trained to kill. His hopes were firmly planted in a militant cult worldview. Trained by Al Qaeda and nurtured by hate, he was transformed into the perfect criminal soldier. The modern face of warfare was changed forever by the success of Atta's team. Atta's letter contains instructions to his team and specific details of how to prepare themselves for their perceived sacred duty. The author will revisit Atta again in "Virus", but for now it is sufficient to allow him to speak for himself. His letter gives the reader a fascinating yet repulsive glimpse into the lethal mind of a suicide operative. It is also important that the reader understand that Atta's actions are not consistent with orthodox Islam.

Atta's Letter

(Released by F.B.I. and translated for The New York Times by Capital Communications Group)

THE LAST NIGHT

1) Making an oath to die and renew your intentions.

Shave excess hair from the body and wear cologne.

Shower

2) Make sure you know all aspects of the plan well, and expect the response, or a reaction, from the enemy.

3) Read al-Tawba and Anfal [traditional war chapters from the Qur'an] and reflect on their meanings and remember all of the things God has promised for the martyrs.

4) Remind your soul to listen and obey [all divine orders] and remember that you will face decisive situations that might prevent you from 100 per cent obedience, so tame your soul, purify it, convince it, make it understand, and incite it. God said: 'Obey God and His Messenger, and do not fight amongst yourselves or else you will fail. And be patient, for God is with the patient.'

5) Pray during the night and be persistent in asking God to give you victory, control and conquest, and that He may make your task easier and not expose us.

6) Remember God frequently, and the best way to do it is to read the Holy Qur'an, according to all scholars, as far as I know. It is enough for us that it [the Qur'an] are the words of the Creator of the Earth and the plants, the One that you will meet [on the Day of Judgment].

7) Purify your soul from all unclean things. Completely forget something called 'this world' [or 'this life']. The time for play is over and the serious time is upon us. How much time have we wasted in our lives? Shouldn't we take advantage of these last hours to offer good deeds and obedience?

8) You should feel complete tranquility, because the time between you and your marriage [in heaven] is very short. Afterwards begins the happy life, where God is satisfied with you, and eternal bliss 'in the company of the prophets, the companions, the martyrs and the good people, who are all good company'. Ask God for his mercy and be optimistic, because [the Prophet], peace be upon him, used to prefer optimism in all his affairs.

9) Keep in mind that, if you fall into hardship, how will you act and how will you remain steadfast and remember that you will return to God and remember that anything that happens to you could never be avoided, and what did not happen to you could never have happened to you. This test from Almighty God is to raise your level [levels of heaven] and erase your sins. And be sure that it is a matter of moments, which will then pass, God willing, so blessed are those who win the great reward of God. Almighty God said: 'Did you think you could go to heaven before God knows whom amongst you have fought for Him and are patient?'

10) Remember the words of Almighty God: 'You were looking to the battle before you engaged in it, and now you see it with your own two eyes.' Remember: 'How many small groups beat big groups by the will of God.' And His words: 'If God gives you victory, no one can beat you. And if He betrays you, who can give you victory without Him? So the faithful put their trust in God.'

11) Remind yourself of the supplications and of your brethren and ponder their meanings. (The morning and evening supplications, and the supplications of [entering] a town, and the [unclear] supplications, and the supplications said before meeting the enemy.

12) Bless your body with some verses of the Qur'an [done by reading verses into one's hands and then rubbing the hands over whatever is to be blessed], the lug-

gage, clothes, the knife, your personal effects, your ID, passport, and all your papers.

13) Check your weapon before you leave and long before you leave. (You must make your knife sharp and must not discomfort your animal during the slaughter).

14) Tighten your clothes [a reference to making sure his clothes will cover his private parts at all times], since this is the way of the pious generations after the Prophet. They would tighten their clothes before battle. Tighten your shoes well, wear socks so that your feet will be solidly in your shoes. All of these are worldly things [that humans can do to control their fate, although God decrees what will work and what won't] and the rest is left to God, the best One to depend on.

15) Pray the morning prayer in a group and ponder the great rewards of that prayer. Make supplications afterwards, and do not leave your apartment unless you have performed ablution before leaving, because the angels will ask for your forgiveness as long as you are in a state of ablution, and will pray for you. This saying of the Prophet was mentioned by An-Nawawi in his book, The Best of Supplications. Read the words of God: 'Did you think that We created you for no reason…' from the Al-Mu'minun Chapter.

THE SECOND STEP

When the taxi takes you to (M) [this initial could stand for matar, airport in Arabic] remember God constantly while in the car. (Remember the supplication for entering a car, for entering a town, the supplication of place and other supplications).

When you have reached (M) and have left the taxi, say a supplication of place ['Oh Lord, I ask you for the best of this place, and ask you to protect me from its evils'], and everywhere you go say that prayer and smile and be calm, for God is with the believers. And the angels protect you without you feeling anything. Say this supplication: 'God is more dear than all of His creation.' And say: 'Oh Lord, protect me from them as You wish.' And say: 'Oh Lord, take your anger out on [the enemy] and we ask You to protect us from their evils.' And say: 'Oh Lord, block their vision from in front of them, so that they may not see.' And say: 'God is all we need, He is the best to rely upon.' Remember God's words: 'Those to whom the people said, "The people have gathered to get you, so fear them," but that only increased their faith and they said, God is all we need, He is the best to rely upon.' After you say that, you will find [unclear] as God promised this to his servants who say this supplication:

1) They will come back [from battle] with God's blessings

2) They were not harmed

3) And God was satisfied with them.

God says: 'They came back with God's blessings, were not harmed, and God was satisfied with them, and God is ever-blessing.'

All of their equipment and gates and technology will not prevent, nor harm, except by God's will. The believers do not fear such things. The only ones that fear it are the allies of Satan, who are the brothers of the devil. They have become their allies, God save us, for fear is a great form of worship, and the only one worthy of it is God. He is the only one who deserves it. He said in the verses: 'This is only the Devil scaring his allies' who are fascinated with Western civilisation, and have drank the love [of the West] like they drink water [unclear] and have become afraid of their weak equipment, 'so fear them not, and fear Me, if you are believers.'

Fear is a great worship. The allies of God do not offer such worship except for the one God, who controls everything. [unclear] with total certainty that God will weaken the schemes of non-believers. God said: 'God will weaken the schemes of the non-believers.'

You must remember your brothers with all respect. No one should notice that you are making the supplication, 'There is no God but God,' because if you say it 1,000 times no one will be able to tell whether you are quiet or remember God. And among its miracles is what the Prophet, peace be upon him, said: 'Whoever says, "There is no God but God," with all his heart, goes to heaven.' The prophet, peace be upon him, said: 'If you put all the worlds and universes on one side of the balance, and "No God but God" on the other, "No God but God" will weigh more heavily.' You can repeat these words confidently, and this is just one of the strengths of these words. Whoever thinks deeply about these words will find that they have no dots [in the Arabic letter] and this is just one of its greatnesses, for words that have dots in them carry less weight than those that do not. And it is enough that these are the words of monotheism, which will make you steadfast in battle [unclear] as the prophet, peace be upon him, and his companions, and those who came after them, God willing, until the Day of Judgment.

Do not seem confused or show signs of nervous tension. Be happy, optimistic, calm because you are heading for a deed that God loves and will accept. It will be the day, God willing, you spend with the women of paradise.

[poetry] Smile in the face of hardship young man/For you are heading toward eternal paradise

You must remember to make supplications wherever you go, and anytime you do anything, and God is with his faithful servants, He will protect them and make their tasks easier, and give them success and control, and victory, and everything…

THE THIRD PHASE

When you ride the (T) [probably for tayyara, aeroplane in Arabic], before your foot steps in it, and before you enter it, you make a prayer and supplications. Remember that this is a battle for the sake of God. As the prophet, peace be upon him, said, 'An action for the sake of God is better than all of what is in this world.' When you step inside the (T), and sit in your seat, begin with the known supplications that we have mentioned before. Be busy with the constant remembrance of God. God said: 'Oh ye faithful, when you find the enemy be steadfast, and remember God constantly so that you may be successful.' When the (T) moves, even slightly, toward (Q) [unknown reference], say the supplication of travel. Because you are traveling to Almighty God, so be attentive on this trip.

Then [unclear] it takes off. This is the moment that both groups come together. So remember God, as He said in His book: 'Oh Lord, pour your patience upon us and make our feet steadfast and give us victory over the infidels.' And His words: 'And the only thing they said Lord, forgive our sins and excesses and make our feet steadfast and give us victory over the infidels.' And His prophet said: 'Oh Lord, You have revealed the book, You move the clouds, You gave us victory over the enemy, conquer them and give us victory over them.' Give us victory and make the ground shake under their feet. Pray for yourself and all your brothers that they may be victorious and hit their targets and ask God to grant you martyrdom facing the enemy, not running away from it, and for Him to grant you patience and the feeling that anything that happens to you is for Him.

Then every one of you should prepare to carry out his role in a way that would satisfy God. You should clench your teeth, as the pious early generations did.

When the confrontation begins, strike like champions who do not want to go back to this world. Shout, 'Allahu Akbar,' because this strikes fear in the hearts of the non-believers. God said: 'Strike above the neck, and strike at all of their extremities.' Know that the gardens of paradise are waiting for you in all their beauty, and the women of paradise are waiting, calling out, 'Come hither, friend of God.' They have dressed in their most beautiful clothing.

If God decrees that any of you are to slaughter, dedicate the slaughter to your fathers and [unclear], because you have obligations toward them. Do not disagree, and obey. If you slaughter, do not cause the discomfort of those you are killing, because this is one of the practices of the prophet, peace be upon him. On one condition: that you do not become distracted by [unclear] and neglect what is greater, paying attention to the enemy. That would be treason, and would do more damage than good. If this happens, the deed at hand is more important than doing that, because the deed is an obligation, and [the other thing] is optional. And an obligation has priority over an option.

Do not seek revenge for yourself. Strike for God's sake. One time Ali bin Abi Talib [a companion and close relative of the prophet Muhammad], fought with a non-believer. The non-believer spit on Ali, may God bless him. Ali [unclear] his sword, but did not strike him. When the battle was over, the companions of the prophet asked him why he had not smitten the non-believer. He said, 'After he spat at me, I was afraid I would be striking at him in revenge for myself, so I lifted my sword.' After he renewed his intentions, he went back and killed the man. This means that before you do anything, make sure your soul is prepared to do everything for God only.

Then implement the way of the prophet in taking prisoners. Take prisoners and kill them. As Almighty God said: 'No prophet should have prisoners until he has soaked the land with blood. You want the bounties of this world [in exchange for prisoners] and God wants the other world [for you], and God is all-powerful, all-wise.'

If everything goes well, every one of you should pat the other on the shoulder in confidence that (M) and (T) number (K). Remind your brothers that this act is for Almighty God. Do not confuse your brothers or distract them. He should give them glad tidings and make them calm, and remind them [of God] and encourage them. How beautiful it is for one to read God's words, such as: 'And those who prefer the afterlife over this world should fight for the sake of God.' And His words: 'Do not suppose that those who are killed for the sake of God are dead; they are alive...' And others. Or they should sing songs to boost their morale, as the pious first generations did in the throes of battle, to bring calm, tranquillity and joy to the hearts of his brothers.

Do not forget to take a bounty, even if it is a glass of water to quench your thirst or that of your brothers, if possible. When the hour of reality approaches, the zero hour, [unclear] and wholeheartedly welcome death for the sake of God. Always be remembering God. Either end your life while praying, seconds before the target, or make your last words: 'There is no God but God, Muhammad is His messenger'.

Afterwards, we will all meet in the highest heaven, God willing.

If you see the enemy as strong, remember the groups [that had formed a coalition to fight the prophet Muhammad]. They were 10,000. Remember how God gave victory to his faithful servants. He said: 'When the faithful saw the groups, they said, this is what God and the prophet promised, they said the truth. It only increased their faith.'

And may the peace of God be upon the prophet.

Lethal Minds: The Creation of a Terrorist Mindset

By H. Hazim

July 2002

This is part of a transcript of a videotape of Usama bin Laden talking with others, translated from Arabic into English. It was released by the U.S. Department of Defense to various news outlets on December 13, 2001.

Usamah bin Laden: We were at a camp of one of the brother's guards in Qandahar. This brother belonged to the majority of the group. He came close and told me that he saw, in a dream, a tall building in America, and in the same dream he saw Mukhtar teaching them how to play karate. At that point, I was worried that maybe the secret would be revealed if everyone starts seeing it in their dream. So I closed the subject. I told him if he sees another dream, not to tell anybody, because people will be upset with him

Introduction

The paper "Lethal Minds: The Creation of a Terrorist Mindset" was constructed to provide sociological intelligence to anyone who works in the field of national security. This group consists of law enforcement, public safety workers, military personnel and security researchers. This author claims sole responsibility for the views expressed. The paper compiles 18 months of research into a 28-page document that is easily read, and the aim is to present an accurate assessment of what could take hold of the youth in Islamic cultures and subcultures (smaller movements in various cultures) if things remain as they are. Radical subcultures can spring up anywhere, even in the US. This fact was well publicized by the coverage that two young Americans received when they fell victim to this type of radicalization. One, John Walker, will face 20 years for assisting the Taliban and the other, Jose Padillia, was arrested for seeking to build a dirty bomb. The crisis concerning radicalization, its reach, and its offspring terrorism, has not yet abated, and words from my earlier paper, "Middle Eastern Interpretation of Jihad and the Far reaching Consequences," are still relevant today.

"Yet several elements remain in the Middle East and they stubbornly adhere to a radical interpretation of scripture showing no tolerance for deviation, and they appear to be growing at an alarming rate. These particular supranational movements use the Quran as their ultimate source of authority, giving rise to different interpretations among different Islamic factions. This leads to a splintering effect that gives rise to dangerous militant groups that are opposed to the authority structures currently in place. These elements continue to build a base while converting people to their version of the faith. It is now a threat that the US is not prepared to deal with and one that Israel has handled poorly. **Since any idea conceptualized and taught to a group can justify**

any act in the name of a cause, one of the greatest challenges to the security of the Middle East and America may be a particular term that Muslims of the world call jihad."[1]

Methodology

The paper is written as part of an ongoing study into the nature of radicals who claim Islam as a religion. It will cover, inadequately, the history of jihad and the beginning of its use during the conquest period of the caliphs, socialization, indoctrination practices, geographical hotbeds, the motivations of the participants, and most importantly, the lethal mindset produced by radicalization. As stated earlier, although the paper *is* interdisciplinary in nature, it draws primarily from a sociological approach.

The sociology of religion and its effects on cultures and subcultures are plainly stated during this study, while most of the more technical language is left out in order to avoid confusing those who are not familiar with the field. It should be noted that radical movements that use religion as a guiding ideology are nothing new, and the author's intention is not to subject orthodox Islam to public scrutiny, because orthodox Islam does not claim the child of extremism; it is disowned in most orthodox circles. The paper is written as an informative/theoretical document that examines the ideas that have caused this version to become a national security issue. The audience it is directed towards includes government, public safety officials and researchers who labor to secure their countries.

Throughout this paper I will also address spiritual containment (the essential role Muslims must play in containing this virus). It is needed, and all clerics of good will must be consulted. I raise the issue here for one major reason, Islam is the leading ideology in Middle Eastern countries and the term jihad is a part of Islam. Therefore, it is of the utmost importance to define jihad in orthodox terms. Orthodox Muslims and fair-minded scholars must assert themselves more, and define jihad before the radical elements of a pseudo faith claim the term exclusively and become the filters of truth for the young, impressionable masses. Keep in mind that this is a paper about one type of terrorism, but the indoctrination aspects can be applied to all forms. The author defines a lethal mind as anyone who supports terrorism. This includes all radicals, teachers, imams, organizers, recruiters, suicide bombers, (and the families that support them) and financial supporters. America must devote time and research into the area of sociological intelligence; it neglects such an endeavor to its own peril.

Section II: Jihad Ideas: The Meaning, History and Perversion of the Word

Jihad today is essentially defined by orthodox Muslims the same way its founder, Muhammad, defined it over 1400 years ago. Over 1400 years later, it is essentially the same thing; something I learned as a child and member of the faith; it was a term defined by one word, struggle. This was a struggle against something internal or external. Jihad was primarily waged internally and against one's lower nature, and this is what the prophet Muhammad called "greater jihad" [Book of Hadith of Al Furqan baina Auliyair Rahman wa Auliyaisy Shaitaan, 44–45]. When waged externally and in terms of war, it allowed for self-defense and the removal of unjust, oppressive regimes. Clearly the word has been perverted, and terrorists, armed with this radical version, are seeking ways to convert the young fertile minds of Muslims everywhere.

The call for jihad against the West, and America in particular, has its roots in more than Western support for Israel. Algerian sociologist, Fatima Mernissi, has a particular take on why certain cultures are prone to receive radical versions of Islam, and reject the West. In her view, many Middle Eastern and Northern African countries have given the West the name of "the Garb" or "al-maghrib al-aqsa" in Arabic, because the values and belief systems of the West are so vastly different than theirs and perceived to be harmful to Islam. When this is coupled with the fear of being overrun with American influence, their political regimes and citizens naturally resist. The Garb is defined as a cursed place, the land of the setting sun, and it takes on mythical proportions for those who have never been here. It is a forbidden place of seduction, material idolatry, and strangeness. It stands for all that is evil and dark in the minds of those inhabiting these cultures.[2] Radical adherents to this view believe that if a culture is poisonous, then every Western civilian should be targeted, because they are carriers of a harmful Western virus that will infect Muslims in their regions. Since terrorists are serious about challenging a global power and culture, their reach has become global. The ideas that justify terrorism on a global scale have not appeared overnight; they have gradually taken root in the fertile grounds of many hostile hearts that are in agreement with the new version of jihad.

Ideas are powerful and a regional jihad against US interests has been in place for the last forty years largely due to the fact that Middle Eastern countries sought to rid themselves of Israel and its primary backer, the US. Global jihad is a more recent development.[3] Redefining Jihad has been moderately successful, and the idea has a fertile womb and the ability to spread in democracies where free speech and technological innovation combine. Historically, democracies have abstained from taking action against ideas until acted upon in ways that violate a nation's laws. Radical groups operate under free speech, and hence remain untouched while the call for jihad thunders over the phone, Internet, television and radio stations. Ideas are powerful, and they can move cultures forward or backwards. Ideas mobilize movements, guide emotions, instigate revolutions, and when fully realized by the masses, they are able to minimize the influence and power of political leaders, or overthrow them altogether. To understand the original idea and intent of a global jihad, one must visit the genesis of jihad activity.

1400 years ago Jihad activity started out regionally, but even during this time Muhammad clearly declared jihad was a basic universal teaching of the Quran. Jihad (meaning all Muslims should struggle against their enemies; their internal desires or lower nature and their external oppressors) was not optional for believers (some Imams claim it was) when the small ummah was under attack (Quran, Sura 4:95). Jihad was thus both peaceful and violent because it was waged internally within one's soul as a means of purification and externally against a physical enemy. Although most of Islam's expansion occurred after the death of Muhammad, the origins of its regional dimensions are clearly laid out by its prophet because he compelled all Muslims to wage a just jihad after 13 years of peaceful resistance to enemies. He offered mercy to his enemies, and many Islamic records demonstrate his efforts towards peace before and after war. His belief that Islam was universal, and its enemies should have an opportunity to embrace it remained with him throughout his life, and this caused him to be patient with his adversaries and place limits on warfare.[4] Muhammad did not institute or sanction the radical jihad seen today; his teachings did not support it. The task of the Islamic community will be recapturing the scriptures through the words and nature of their prophet.

Muhammad was first of all a deeply religious man. He was a simple, humble, illiterate man given to retreating to caves for a time of fasting and meditation. The aim of his call was primarily a religious one. The call to become a prophet began when, according to Muhammad, the angel Gabriel appeared to him and commanded him to *iqrah* (read). (This is the famous 96th Sura in the Quran that summoned Muhammad to the call of a prophet.) Muhammad replied he could not, and once again the visitor commanded him to, "Read in the name of Him Who created man from a congealed clot of blood."[5] Subsequent encounters that produced revelation were written down, and many became part of the *Holy Quran*. Muslims who hold to the view that every word was given directly to Muhammad revere the Quran. Muhammad's claims of divine authority caused him to be persecuted in his day. As his popularity spread and threatened the powers of the day, he and his followers were attacked and some were killed.

Muhammad suffered at the hands of his enemies for 13 years before he authorized the use of armed resistance. Afterwards, the prophet would allow his people to engage in warfare during times of persecution or great oppression. He preached that, "Oppression is worse than death." (Sura 2: 191.23). Yet when he commanded the believers to resist, even oppressors were given mercy and most Muslim scholars attest to this view of historical Islam. In addition, Muhammad laid out several guidelines for warfare that were not to be transgressed. Ralph Salmi's book, *Islam and Conflict Resolution,* is a valuable resource for anyone interested in jihad, and it documents the principles Muhammad laid out for jihad as agreed upon by most orthodox Islamic jurists, scholars and clerics.

Acts permitted by jihad {List taken From **Ralph Salmi's** book, *Islam and Conflict Resolution*}

1. Enemy combatants can be killed, wounded, captured and pursued. Noncombatants could not be killed, unless they served as advisors to the enemy and caused danger to Muslims.
2. Ruses and ambushes can be resorted to in order to cause confusion and the defeat of the enemy.
3. Propaganda may be used to demoralize the enemy or cause some of them to convert to the Islamic side. False news is also appropriate in this setting.
4. The enemy can be attacked with different types of weapons. (There are some disagreements among jurists concerning the use of poison arrows)
5. Assassination of top leaders is also permissible if it serves the purpose of lessening the amount of bloodshed.
6. If the enemy uses innocent people (Civilians, elderly, children, Muslims, and women) as human shields, Muslims are still allowed to attack, but they must take as much caution as possible not to harm the innocent.
7. Enemy property can be captured or destroyed.
8. The enemy's water supply can be cut off.
9. Food and fodder from the enemy can be requisitioned for the Muslim army's use (providing the food is consistent with Islamic diet).
10. Night attacks
11. Hostile inhabitants can be fined or imprisoned.
12. Muslim relief work can also be performed for humanitarian purposes.

Acts prohibited during jihad {Chart taken From Ralph Salmi's book, *Islam and Conflict Resolution*}

1. The killing of noncombatants
2. Cruel ways of killing (torture and methods that prolong death)
3. Execution of prisoners of war
4. Severing heads and sending them to higher authorities
5. Mutilation of man and beast
6. Unnecessary devastation of the enemy's land, destruction of harvest, and the unnecessary cutting of trees
7. Adultery or fornication with female captives
8. Killing enemy hostages
9. Massacre of innocents
10. Killing of one's parents who belong to the enemy's camp, except in cases of self-defense
11. Killing of traders, merchants, peasants and others engaged in peaceful occupations
12. Using enemy prisoners as shields or compelling them to fight their former army
13. Violating treaty agreements.
14. Retaliation when they kill Muslim women, children, the aged and hostages
15. Retaliation for mutilation [6]

When the facts of how a jihad is to be conducted are viewed, it becomes obvious that terrorists do not understand jihad and reinterpret history for their own ends.

To understand the motivations of terrorists and the moral legitimacy they seek, one must look at how they view Islamic history. Their view of history always includes a caliph, which means successor to the prophet. All of the first four caliphs personally knew Muhammad before his death and succeeded him and each other in turn. Many terrorists believe the caliph was not just the answer for the Islamic community during that time but for all time. Abu Bakr, 'Umar, Uthman and Ali are called the "Rightly Guided Caliphs" by Sunnis (dominant branch of professing Muslims, Sunnis, but the Shiites believe that Ali was the only legitimate successor of the four) largely due to their association with the prophet, their military and political success, and their ability stomp out apostasy.[7] Terrorists seek to establish themselves on a historical basis by aligning themselves with the caliphate. They seek to implement their version of true Islam, and the ignorant and deluded follow these interpretations of jihad and Islam, interpretations spun by the inexplicable lies of terrorists.

The caliph could declare jihad against unbelievers and believers alike for the purposes of self-defense, conquest or to squash apostasy, but after the death of the last of the four "Rightly Guided Caliphs" an even greater perversion of the word set in. In fact, any political leader could declare jihad as long as he had the support of an imam, and such support was easily gained. During the reign of the first four caliphs, imams were consulted, but the caliph was not required to do so because he held the title of imam as well. The first four caliphs were supported because the ummah (community) believed the caliph was the legitimate sole authority over the community, and because of this belief he was revered as the embodiment of spiritual and political authority. Some Muslims yearn for the simplicity of that order today, and they believe that a jihad against apostate regimes and unbelievers is necessary to return Islam to its former glory.[8]

The expansion of Islam and its use of jihad were very effective after the death of Muhammad. Two factors contributed to the political manipulation of jihad: the death of Muhammad brought about a vacuum that needed to be filled by a competent leader while the military successes of the caliphs brought about a rapid conversion rate among Arabs, which gave rise to a unity previously unthinkable. Since Muhammad consolidated both spiritual and civil authority into his hands, his followers saw no need to change this model; therefore, the title of Caliph Bakr was first given to Abu Bakr. He lived out the remainder of his life with the title Caliph Bakr. The last three caliphs, 'Umar, Uthman and Ali, were not so fortunate; they were all assassinated. This new empire had internal and external enemies, and disgruntled subjects or colleagues assassinated three of the first four caliphs. Two of the assassins justified their actions by calling the caliph an apostate.[9] Terrorist leaders call for an overthrow of apostate leaders through violence by espousing the same type of ideology that caused the caliphs' deaths.

The purpose in the warfare of the four Caliphs was somewhat at odds with the original intentions of Muhammad and encouraging conversion included threats of death, imprisonment, or taxation, which, led to some of the internal problems of the young empire.[10] Some of the practices of the caliphs, especially the Apostate Wars, did not square with the statement "Islam is not a compulsory religion" (Quran, Sura 2:256). The more aggressive interpretation of jihad was used for expansion and was similar to the Western idea of "Manifest Destiny." This was no accident but intentional, old-fashioned realism and political opportunism. Jihad was used often during warfare and conflict as a political tool after the Caliphs as well, but for purposes of this paper we will focus on the recent resurgence of the word. Jihad entered Western consciousness with great force in the late seventies enduring through the eighties. The new impetus for the use of jihad against enemies was found in Afghanistan.

Afghanistan, USSR, America and the New Jihadists

Perhaps the biggest motivation for this new supranational movement occurred when the USSR put into practice the Brezhnev doctrine, the doctrine stated once a Soviet republic always a Soviet republic. This was done without considering the consequences. The use of force against the Afghans caused a swirl of support to occur in Islamic countries and the deep pockets of the US military saw the opportunity for payback for their losses in Vietnam, but neither the US nor the Soviets realized the hydra they were creating. This game of chess between the two superpowers helped to produce some of what is seen today. The US helped fund, supply and train the Mujahideen without enough sagacity and the USSR gave the supranational force a common enemy to rally against. Both nations gave jihadists the belief that they could take on a superpower and win.

The USSR made a critical mistake when it invaded Afghanistan, and the frustration of countless Muslims was vented in this war, causing some to take up arms. For its part, the US was overly concerned about the opportunity to hurt the Soviet Union and was not farsighted enough. Many devout Muslims flocked from all over the world to participate in jihad, but many radicals appeared as well. When the US began to aid the Mujahideen with stingers and other weapons the tide of the war changed. Unfortunately, many radicals began to interpret this as God's providence, and Afghanistan became a rallying cry for fighters to throw off the weight of foreign oppression and intrusion. To call or appeal for a jihad against your enemies became a logical and appropriate response to a perceived threat. This idea would be exported through the various channels of communication in the Islamic world, and religious leaders were the primary spokesmen.

For the first time a global jihad could be fought, and Abdullah Azzam soon emerged as a candidate to lead a new global jihad movement. He was arguably the most influential scholar in the new jihad movement, and he died as a participant (martyr to many) in the Afghan war. He wrote several booklets including, "Join the Caravan," which called for Muslims everywhere to come to the aid of oppressed Muslims whenever they knew of them. He was also a mentor for Usamah bin Laden. Azzam was a native Palestinian who grew disenchanted with the PLO due to irreligious motivations on the part of the leadership. He stated that many within the leadership claimed the Palestinian struggle had nothing to do with Islam, and this infuriated him, causing him to leave for Egypt, where he earned a Ph.D. in Islamic studies. He remained there to teach in some of the various universities until the jihad in Afghanistan.[11]

Three reasons explain why Azzam became so popular: he was Palestinian, and the Palestinian struggle has often been a rallying point for the Arabic and Islamic world, he participated physically in jihad, and he was the most articulate of the new jihadists. Numerous people fought in this war, but Azzam was exceptional in his leadership and scholarship. His ideas were published and they helped start a movement that called for a more robust interpretation of jihad in Islamic lands ruled by corrupt dictators who he viewed as puppets of the West. The victories in Afghanistan emboldened many of his followers, and he outlined 8 reasons why Muslims should participate bodily in jihad. His booklet, "Join the Caravan" lists the following reasons:

1. In order that the disbelievers do not dominate
2. Due to the scarcity of men
3. Fear of hellfire
4. Fulfilling the duty of jihad
5. Following the footsteps of the Pious Predecessors (Salafi: First three generations after the prophet)
6. Establishing a solid foundation for the base of Islam
7. Protecting those who are oppressed in the land
8. Hoping for Martyrdom[12]

[These are the main reasons behind jihad participation, but numbers 3 and 8 are the vinegar and honey set before everyone recruited for this cause. Although the true aim of the Mujahideen lies in hoping for martyrdom, the fear of hell fire is frequently cited in radical literature, yet under appreciated and seldom spoken of in the West. For those who participate in jihad, the promise of heaven is appealing, but the thought of a continued miserable life here and hell afterwards is terrifying. This will be explored in more detail in section three of this paper.]

Keep in mind the US did not consider Azzam a terrorist, but rather a freedom fighter waging a legitimate jihad in orthodox terms and based on regional aims, but soon he became a supranationalist. (A supranationalist is someone who fights for a universal cause and extends the fighting beyond any borders, and his fighting is usually based on religion.) He called for Muslims to unite, and rise up wherever oppression existed. Many then and now are continuing to "Join the Caravan." Materialistic motivations fall short of describing the zeal of supranationalists like Azzam, Bin Laden, Mohammad Atta, and the numerous foreign fighters in places like Pakistan, Chechnya and Afghanistan. (Afghanistan let numerous supranational fighters go during the early phases of the US campaign there, and they will surface again.) There is a difference between the two camps, and this paper will explore this in more detail in section four, but regional radicalism is responsible for introducing one form of a lethal mind that suprantionalists use, the suicide bomber.

Regional radicalism in Palestine and Lebanon popularized suicide bombings. Keep in mind, Palestinian and Hezbollah terrorism and their popular and effective tactic of suicide bombing is an indicator of the lengths a lethal mind is willing to go. Regional jihad studies shed light on some of the motivations of jihad participants. Their common links with all young, impressionable bombers are a desire of vengeance, freedom from foreign intrusion, and religious gratification. Men like Daniel Williams who wrote an article titled, "Suicide Bombers Nurtured by Despair", head the list of one school of thought, oppression politics. The article highlighted what Palestinian researchers have concluded about the root of this problem; it's Israel. The researchers did not interview the poor and uneducated; they interviewed college students. "We found that our students generally have an inability to dream, or to visualize a better future than their miserable current life."[13] The article blamed the phenomenon of suicide bombings on poverty, apartheid, and injustice on the part of Israel, and hopelessness. Although this may explain part of the problem, the author of this study views these conclusions as inadequate, because the problems of poverty and occupation exist in other areas of the globe, but the phenomena of suicide operations are not found there, and if so, they are not nearly as prevalent. Terrorist organizations needed to develop a cult like obedience from followers before they could wage this type of asymmetric warfare.

Terrorist organizations needed new weapons. The weapons would be used against Islamic regimes, Israel and America; thus, the suicide bombers were created, giving terrorists a weapon that could not be defeated. They were created and in clear contradiction to Islamic principles. With the onset of these new bombers a far more radical and dangerous form of Islam emerged, and it gave the movement the military power and political power it so desperately craved. Previously, Western influence was attempting to win the battle for the hearts and minds of the youth in these countries, but suddenly a new aggressive brand of faith began to spread and to the surprise of many moderate Muslims, one amazingly appealing to the youth who they believed were more interested in the ways of the West. The clerics that supported this movement began to win support from ardent followers, and they were the leaders of resistance to Western influence. To date, the resistance continues, and with these factors currently in place, social scientists and security experts have predicted persistent unrest for these regions. Their conclusions are based on the continuing struggle between two groups with two schools of thought. One seeks reform that will produce increased secularism, and the other adherence to their version of shariah (Islamic law).[14]

Terrorists have redefined jihad and frequently cite Islamic laws and the various interpretations of it when they attempt to articulate the motivations behind their acts. The idea of radical jihad, both regionally and supranationally, is often used to justify attacks on civilians and soldiers alike. Even though jihad is based on two levels of warfare: greater= war with the self, and lesser= war with the oppressor, terrorists actively distort this and remain self-deluded about their own righteousness. Their interpretation encourages violence against civilians.[15] Terrorists seek to incite the masses against the US and Israel. The US must use caution. Every imprudent action on the part of America will prove to be the equivalent of Hercules' blade against the many heads of the hydra, giving rise to another convert or another terrorist group. Such groups and their interpretations do not arise independent of the organizations that nurture, encourage and financially support such radicalism. These organizations will be addressed in the next section.

Section III: Mass Production of Lethal Minds: Socialization, Indoctrination and the Role of Clerics

Note: The terms socialization and indoctrination will be used selectively, not interchangeably. Socialization is defined as the way human beings acquire culture or subcultures. Members living in a particular culture or subculture have learned to accept and follow certain beliefs. Once people are born in a culture and raised according to its values, they are socialized into fixed worldviews because various institutions already in place have taught them, and some cultures have a terrorist society due to reasons of socialization. This is why the Bush administration wants the Palestinians to choose new leadership. Indoctrination is defined slightly differently in this study; it is used to describe the process of teaching and instilling the beliefs of one particular group to others who have voluntarily submitted to this group; however, if indoctrination is to be successful several previous socialized beliefs must be in place. An example would be the socialized belief in heaven used to teach the believer that he must do certain things to get there. A skilled indoctrinator would likely use socialized beliefs to his own advantage and end; however, it is more difficult to indoctrinate those who have not been

socialized in a certain culture. There are other definitions for indoctrination, but I am limiting the use of the word to voluntary participation in this study. The author believes that religious indoctrination cannot occur without the voluntary submission of those instructed, and participants who are willingly indoctrinated cannot claim brainwashing as a defense; they must be held accountable because they are willingly taking part in their own radicalization.

The mosque, masjid, temple, madrasah, church and other sacred places can easily be transformed from a place of worship and education to a training place of terror, depending on the leadership and the methods used to socialize or indoctrinate. Some students seek these places out and volunteer to be radicalized, (this is indoctrination) while others are socialized into this. Through neglect or active support, statesmen and religious leaders in Palestine, Pakistan, Afghanistan, Iran, Lebanon and Saudi Arabia have produced pockets in their culture destined to radicalize the young. Socialization cannot occur outside the context of a culture, and culture is the product of the various institutions that shape it. When the leading institutions in a culture embrace or tolerate Islamic radicalism, the culture becomes lost and headed for perdition. Those who are drawn to these cultures and wish to be indoctrinated seek out the various institutions that exist in these places and indoctrination will follow when individuals choose to immerse themselves in certain teachings posted on leaflets, written in booklets, or made accessible online.

The socialization and indoctrination process can cause a person to lose sight of logic and bolster an individual's determination to unheard of depths of commitment in an effort to carry out God's mission. This process is so effective and has become so far reaching, that even college educated students, such as John Walker, some of the September 11th attackers, and several Palestinian suicide soldiers chose this option for their future. Keep in mind that there are tens of thousands like them who are willing and ready to make the ultimate sacrifice, and their numbers are growing. Excerpts from John Burns's article illustrate this. In "Martyrdom: The Promise of Paradise that Slays Peace" he highlights the problem now confronting militaries with superior technology when they are faced with soldiers who prefer death to life.

> But in no other religion, in modern times, has the cult of martyrdom taken root as it has in Islam, even though moderate Islamic scholars argue that the

Quranic injunction to seek Paradise by dying in battle with the infidel does not extend to acts premised on suicide…
Scholars have traced the tradition of martyrdom to the beginnings of the faith, in seventh-century Arabia, when the Prophet Muhammad led his followers in battle, teaching them, according to a verse from the Koran, to wage aggressive war against infidels: "When the sacred months are past, then kill the idolaters wherever you find them." Thus inspired, Arab armies fighting for Islam conquered much of the Middle East and North Africa within a century of the prophet's death…

From the beginning, the Arab warriors struck terror into their enemies with their fearlessness. This, too, was engendered by their faith, which promised those falling in battle instant transport to Paradise. In passages from the Koran and other Islamic scriptures that are hand-copied on scraps of paper and carried into combat by Muslim fighters in the contemporary wars in Afghanistan, Chechnya, Somalia and a score of other spots, the rewards of martyrdom make anything the Romans envisaged in their Elysian fields seem tame…

The Delights proscribed for Muslims on Earth, Muslim fighters are encouraged to believe, will be theirs in the afterlife if they win the status of shaheed, or martyr. In some versions the delights include the sweetest of wines and unlimited sex with the 72 virgins, lovely as rubies, with complexions like diamonds and pearls, who are the martyrs' promised reward. "Therein shall they delight themselves, lying on green cushions and beautiful carpets," the Muslim holy book says…

For the truth of this, it is necessary only to venture into the martyrs' cemetery south of Tehran, where tens of thousands of soldiers who died in the Iran-Iraq war a generation ago lie buried, the flags of martyrdom flapping on staves beside the graves. Even though the war itself, and its ghastly scale of loss, is remembered by many Iranians with little, if any, enthusiasm, every Friday whole families gather beside the graves to picnic, many remembering sons and brothers who were only children when they died. Far from grieving, the mood is mostly one of joy, for the happy souls transported to Paradise[16].

The roots of modern day terrorism are not limited to Islam, and it can be argued persuasively that most historical terrorist activities have their roots in some form of religion. Unfortunately, the radical version of Islam has developed a virtual monopoly on modern religious terrorism, but other faiths have had their share of radicals who were motivated by rewards in the hereafter.

Religious terrorism as a *successful* asymmetric strategy started perhaps 2000 thousand years ago when Jewish zealots specialized in dagger slayings of Roman soldiers and Jewish collaborators. These men had their radical Rabbis. This was followed by the massacres during the Crusades in Jerusalem by Catholic armies; roughly a hundred years later the Assassins killed numerous Crusaders and civilians with their campaigns in what is now Syria and Iran. These Shiites were fully committed to their cause. The Indian example is found in the Thugis. They worshipped the goddess of destruction, Kali, and Kali blessed them with 1200 years of uninterrupted terror campaigns against their enemies. In all of the cases each member of the sect swore an allegiance that was binding till death, and all believed that their work was divinely inspired and would lead to paradise.[17] The pursuit of paradise has been widely documented. This theme is consistent throughout the history of warfare, and it has found a resting place once again in counterfeit Islam. A view of Pakistan will reveal one geographical location for the culture of radicalism and instruments of radicalization.

Pakistan's Madrasahs

Ben Barber is a State Department correspondent for the Washington Times, and his article, "Pakistan's Jihad Factories", sheds light on the upcoming generation of radicals. The word "madrasah" is defined as a religious school or education center. Although it is not a public school, it educates most of the youth in Pakistan because public schools are too expensive for most Pakistanis. There are over 7000 Madrasahs in Pakistan and Saudi Arabia; other Gulf nations, and wealthy Muslim citizens from around the world primarily fund them.[18] The author also highlights some alarming statistics concerning the sheer numbers of those enrolled.

Terrorism's Fertile Garden

There are approximately 10,000 madrasahs (religious schools) in Pakistan, serving 1.75 million students.

The major topic of study is jihad (holy war). Little else is studied but the Quran, which is memorized in the original Arabic.

All students expect to fight in wars against infidels in places such as Chechnya, the Philippines, Afghanistan, and Kashmir.

Parents send their children to these schools because of both their strong religious convictions and their poverty. The schools provide free education, housing, and regular meals.

Saudi Arabia, other Persian Gulf nations, and Muslims in America fund the madrasahs.

> There are now over 3,000 mosques and madrasahs in the United States, according to a Pakistani religious leader who sees them as a force to convert America to Islam[19] {Note: above citation taken unaltered from Barber article}

What started out as an indigenous school for Pakistanis has now spread to US soil, and the ideology has spread. Pakistan produced the previous reign of oppression in Afghanistan by training the Taliban (seminarians). The fact that these seminarians coddled terrorists is no surprise to those who watched the development of the Taliban movement. The madrasahs were there; the clerics were there, and so were the governments of Pakistan, Saudi Arabia and several Gulf states. These nations contributed to the creation of the Taliban regime through their economic resources. Ultimately, it was the madrasahs that produced the collective lethal mind of a regime that produced a state that became the center of terrorism in the world.[20] This mindset became all encompassing and permeated the thinking of the participants until they strove for an idealistic Islamic state headed by a caliph that ruled over a righteous Ummah. These new jihadists dedicated their lives to extremism and their version of jihad; their zeal is unceasing. The pursuit of jihad and subsequent martyrdom is taught in radical madrasahs. Jessica Stern amplifies these points when she made the following observations in her article, "Pakistan's Jihad Culture."

> As some irregulars are financially dependent on what they consider jihad, others are spiritually and psychologically so. Many irregulars who fought in Afghanistan are now fighting in Kashmir and are likely to continue looking for new "jihads" to fight—even against Pakistan itself. Khalil, who has been a "mujahid" for 19 years and can no longer imagine another life, told me, "A person addicted to heroin can get off it if he really tries, but a mujahid cannot leave the jihad. I am spiritually addicted to jihad." Another Harkat operative told me, We won't stop—even if India gave us Kashmir....We'll [also] bring jihad here. There is already a movement here to make Pakistan a pure Islamic state. Many preach Islam, but most of them don't know what it means. We want to see a Taliban-style regime here....but America must do more than just scold. After all, the United States, along with Saudi Arabia, helped create the first international "jihad" to fight the Soviet Union during the Afghan war. "Does America expect us to send in the troops and shut the madrasahs down?" one official asks. "Jihad is a mindset. It developed over many years during the Afghan war. You can't change a mindset in 24 hours."[21]

After socialization or indoctrination, the youth look for ways to validate themselves by pursuing the glory of bloodshed found in jihad activity. As stated earlier, indoctrination is not the same as brainwashing, it is voluntary, and the participant believes that he is in fact getting something for his participation. Martyrdom is openly celebrated in these cultures and not limited to Palestine. The feeling of religious fervor fills the air when the bodies or pictures of suicide bombers are paraded openly during funerals.[22]

The Masjid and the Cleric

Keep in mind the masjid, better known as the mosque, is not a madrasah; it is a place of worship and devotion, a place where one performs service to Allah. The masjid is far less formal and encompasses all of the various branches of Islam. The madrasah is much more formal and comprised of younger students, who volunteer for religious service, and a teacher who is usually an Imam. Madrasahs are located primarily in Central Asia, the Middle East and the West, including America. Masjids are not geographically limited like madrasahs; they are in fact everywhere you have an Islamic population. A Masjid may be a small barn with a congregation of 15 meeting in Kentucky, to a one hundred million dollar building that can seat thousands. It is often in the smaller Islamic communities where radicalization can take place and a handful of believers select their personal Imam.

According to Sunni Islam, a community of peers must appoint an Imam. This requirement is fine when learned believers participate in the process. Problems arise when less knowledgeable members of the faith participate in the process and vote for questionable leaders by allowing the cult of personality to take over. Many charismatic people without formal training are motivated by their own agenda and seek this title for themselves, or their followers place it upon them. The more radical strains of this type of faith have imams that consider jihad an intricate part of worship and service thus rendering all other acts secondary. The following insert was taken from a website before September 11, and the question of jihad and suicide operations was directed towards a cleric, a particularly devout one who holds the title of Sheik. The question of the curious Muslim is raised, and it is answered.

Attacking the enemy by blowing oneself up

> Question: There are those who tie a magazine of explosives around their waist, then they enter a government or residential building or a gathering of people

either kuffaar or other than them, then they blow themselves up, so what is the ruling regarding this? And is something like this act considered an aspect of valo, and is the one doing so considered a shaheed (martyr) or one who has committed suicide (muntahir)?

Response: No doubt on the face of it he is one who has committed suicide, whereby he has made certain he will be killing himself before anyone else. However, this can be permissible if he is in warring kuffaar territory, and knows he will sooner or later be killed at the hands of the enemy, or will face severe torture and has not found any ploy except to blow himself up and kill others from the enemy (who subject the Muslims to torture) along with himself. In doing so, killing a number of them thereby weakening their strength/ force and reducing their harm and scaring them. So this can be permissible even if it involves killing the person himself, if he knows he will certainly be killed, or persecuted and wishes to rid himself of their harm and attain ease for himself, and his matter is with Allah the Almighty.[23]

These statements are troubling and with good reason. Although the cleric does not particularly encourage the act, he does give his approval of this practice and tactic. He cites the torture and mistreatment of Muslims at the hands of apostate regimes as a reason for suicide operations legitimacy. The youth get a double dose of radicalism when the educational system of some Islamic regimes and the religious centers of worship preach the same brand. Most clerics are not recruiting people for radical jihad, but when clerics excuse and condone the practice by stating that the matter should be left between God and the individual, they become part of the problem.[24]

Some clerics, especially those who have bodily participated in jihad, are clearly recruiting for this purpose by attempting to create a legitimate religion out of the perversion of Islam. Scholarly perversions of the texts, Quran and Hadiths, have become foundational in recruiting the young and maintaining a devout following for terrorists. Terrorists insist that their version is the only legitimate form of the religion, and they know it is impossible to secure the support of the young without conveying a deep personal sense of righteousness that is demonstrated through courageous acts of jihad, and many field commanders are Imams as well. When jihad activity becomes the measure of spirituality, many bloodthirsty individuals have an opportunity to be spiritual. The ties that men develop with their field generals run deep, and when that is coupled with spiritual leadership, the devotion often becomes fanatical.

Western, materialistic bias in conflict studies led to an under appreciation of the role of religious doctrine in warfare before September 11. This is now changing, and resources should be directed towards this study. Research that probes into the indoctrination and socialization process of religious fanaticism is cutting edge research badly needed in today's conflict. It is a sure bet that the religious doctrine of terrorists will change to suit their needs on the battlefield, but it will remain close enough to the original form so that the young will recognize it and be encouraged to join jihad.[25]

Radical clerics consider jihad an obligation, not as voluntary, and they require it of all their followers. The youth in all cultures look for direction and spiritual leadership, and terrorists exploit this. The Old Testament prophet Micah prepared his listeners for his words by stating, "And what does the Lord your God require of You O man?"[26] Extremists use the same approach when they prepare their listeners for statements of requirement. Those who reject the requirements are in danger of hell. Western writers who cite Quranic passages often highlight the rewards of heaven as a reason for jihad, but none of this would be possible without a profound sense of hell that is used to motivate the youth.[27] The motivation of fear is salient in the mind of participants as well.

A View from Iran

Effective indoctrination requires the background and the support of previously held beliefs that have been socialized into a person and are based on hope and fear. The fear of eternal torment and the hope of paradise must be socialized into the hearts and minds of the listeners before indoctrination can take place. Fear must provide the impetus for action, and once a person is convinced he is bound for hell, the certainty of paradise comes into play, but he is only given one option to attain it...sacrifice his life in jihad. This tactic is used over and over again. Most branches are in agreement concerning the reality of hell, although some disagree concerning the length of its duration. The terrors of hell are clearly spelled out in the Quran. It is eternal, and it is not much different from the traditional view of hell that most Christians share. Clerics often dangle their followers over the fires of hell to shake them free from their addiction to the love of this life. Long periods of time are devoted to the subject; this has a powerful psychological effect on the young. According to some Shiite interpretations of shariah, the fighting age for many male children can be as young as 10. This account is taken from a 26 year-old Iranian man named Akbar (Alias, not real name) here in Southern California. He described an incident that took place when he was recruited for the Iran/Iraq war.

They spent about two hours describing the torments of hell in great detail, and it was terrifying. All I wanted to do was escape it. The eyes of the young men widened with surprise and horror. Next they told us we cold escape the fire during a two to five second span of suffering, because death would quickly overtake us on the battlefield. I knew my family would soon be going to America. (I was also told America was the great Satan, and God will destroy it, so I did not tell anyone for fear of being labeled.) I did not want to go to war and not have this opportunity. I watched this as they began to search the eyes of my friends at our school. Next they talked about defeating Iraq. At first they called for volunteers and told us if we did not have the courage to come forward we would not be allowed into paradise; if we were forced to go and fight against our will, there was no guarantee of paradise either. Many stepped forward that day and without their parent's knowledge. I refused, but many of my friends did. I was 11 at the time and some were older than me, a few younger. As they came forward they hung cheap, wooden keys to the gates of paradise around their necks.

They would be on the front lines, and others would clear minefields, others would conduct suicide operations, and few would return. It disgusted me at first, but later I regretted not going because I was viewed as a coward. To this day I am proud to be Muslim and from Iran, and a Shiite. What Americans do not understand is this, most people from the Middle East are not afraid of death; we are use to fighting, killing and being killed. Allah does not permit us to be cowards; we will gladly spill our blood for insult and reproach, let alone our land. So even though I am glad I did not fight, at times I bear the shame of being considered a coward by others.[28]

The man who spoke during the Years of the Iran/Iraq War to Akbar and his classmates were Shiites and one was an Ayatollah. They prepared them to face two certainties: death, which comes to all men, but not necessarily of their choosing, and hell for their cowardly refusal to join jihad. We were told, "If one shirks their duty the frown of the Almighty would rest upon them, and there would be no rest in this life or the next. The curse of Allah was invoked upon anyone who does not do His will, and we were told we must obey our Ayatollahs as His representatives on earth."[29] One must not dismiss the weight of what Akbar has said. When the desire for rewards in the next life is juxtaposed against the fear of eternal torment, most choose eternal life. The Ayatollah firmly reminded them of these things, and soon Iran was extending its influence into Lebanon and corrupting that culture with a new brand of faith. One man personally experienced this. I will call him by the initials N.B. It made him bitter towards Islam in general. He knew; he was there, and he saw the seeds of Hezbollah poisoning.

Radicalization in Lebanon

N.B. was raised as a Catholic in Lebanon and was daily ridiculed by many Lebanese children as both a traitor to his faith and a seed of Satan. Even though he was born in Lebanon, his family was forced to deal with insults and pay more money for goods because they were not believers, and many times he was told he should be stoned to death for his families rejection of Allah. It was considered unnatural for an Arab to be anything other than a Muslim. He was well aware of the support that the Hezbollah received from Iran and what they were doing in the name of religion. "The people hailed them as heroes, and many parents gave their children in hopes that they would be worthy of jihad. What I witnessed was a religion that did not resemble other faiths at all. Although I always disagreed with the basic tenets of Islam, this new version was intolerable of others, violent, and void of compassion towards anyone but their own supporters."[30] This interview was conducted on November 18, 2001 and N.B also had this to say about the September 11 attacks: "All of the talk about Shia Islam being a religion of peace and tolerance is just propaganda. It seeks to dominate all of the various branches of society, culture, education, and politics. I have seen it first hand; it is more political than it is religious."[31] N.B. had some strong words about the faith he experienced in Lebanon and the culture it produced. The Arabian Peninsula has an intolerant culture of its own and produces its own offspring.

Intolerance in Saudi Arabia

Abdul Wahab believed that the legal guardians of the holy places in Islam are always duty bound to guard what is sacred, and he took this seriously. His teachings have socialized most Arabians to be intolerant. Over two centuries ago, this austere student/cleric decided to use his influence and knowledge of Islam to rid the Arabic Bedouins of Sufi and other unorthodox practices. Sufis and Shiites were less strict in their adherence to the faith and combined pagan practices and philosophies with Islam in his opinion. Sufis believed that visiting the tombs of deceased relatives and saints was allowable in Islam, and that visiting a certain number of the tombs of saints would substitute for the Hajj. (A visit to Mecca is something every able bodied Muslim must do at least once in their lifetime.) Sufis taught Muslims that they could do a number of other things that Wahab considered forbidden by the Quran.[32] Wahab decided to put an end to such practices and was successful in doing so and creating an austere version of the faith. This version became the only one that mattered for many of his followers, and eventually its austere practices were at odds with other branches of the faith.

In the early 20th century the Royal Saudi family adopted Wahabism as the state religion, and state law enforced it.

After the emergence of oil in the late 60s and 70s, the exportation of Wahabism became foreign policy. Not only did the Saudis want to build oil lines through Central Asia, they wanted to unite the Central Asians under their version of Islam. This version demanded allegiance and would not tolerate two things: innovation and itjihad, struggling to uncover the truth of a text, or its accurate interpretation. Innovation means new approaches to performing religious service, and itjihad means subjecting the scriptures and Hadiths to ongoing scholarly interpretation. The Saudis could be fairly confident their version of Islam would not undergo any changes as long as Wahabism was followed, and they spent millions of dollars exporting their doctrine and clerics abroad. This began to pay dividends as they helped set up schools in Pakistan, Afghanistan, Great Britain and the US.[33]

Here is one eyewitness account of Wahabism at work. "It was about 2:00 pm in the afternoon, and we saw a large gathering of people. I asked what was happening. I looked up and saw a tall building with two men standing there. They were being forced off at gunpoint, and soon they leapt or were pushed to their death. I asked for the reason, and someone told me they were apostates or something to that effect."[34] Here is another quote from a Southern Californian who left Saudi Arabia upon his conversion to another faith. "When I turned 21 I had to leave because I no longer believed in the Quran, and I knew what happened to anyone who was no longer a Muslim, or to someone who left Wahabism; they were taken to prison upon their confession or sentenced to death. I had witnessed at least two dozen cases since my childhood. I left when I abandoned the faith."[35] A former Gulf War veteran recounts his experiences there and the punishment meted out to transgressors. "It seems like all of the police there, and the people for that matter, were very intolerant towards anything innovative or new. I witnessed people being pulled from their car and beaten, women being slapped, apparently by religious police and elders because their faces were not covered enough, several public executions for what we consider misdemeanors or no crime at all, and an overall feeling of dread. I would never want to live there, unless I was in power."[36]

The author believes, along with others, that a strong program of both propaganda and resocialization programs should be put in place both openly and clandestinely. NGOs can be of use in this region where indoctrination practices and socialization are continuing to claim the hearts and minds of the youth. These must be used to sufficiently counter the growing threat of radicalism. There is no doubt, radical interpretations have become religions in their own right, and although they may not have the following that orthodox branches have, it is possible that the youth in Islamic nations hungering for a more active role in their government may embrace violence in the guise of religion.

Section IV: Jihad's Supranational Appeal: A Recruiting Goldmine and A Nation's Nightmare

The distinction between radical regional jihad (regionally based) and radical supranational jihad (jihad that seeks to unite all believers against all unbelievers) has not been sufficiently explored and in addition, supranationalists have found a gold mine among the young due to the internet and leaderless resistance tactics. Historically, the youth have always been willing cannon fodder, and supranationalists are tapping into this. In this study, jihadists who fight for their homelands and attempt to overthrow regimes within their borders while spending most of their resources and wealth to that end are considered regionalists while those who fight in the name of a universal faith and Ummah (community) are considered supranationalists. Although the lines blur at times and most regionalists consider the US to be a threat to their existence, they are primarily concerned with their own regions, while supranationalists seek ways to attack America, Israel, apostate regimes and Western interests everywhere they can.

The origins of modern supranationalism started with the discovery of oil in the Arab world, and Pan Arabism began to flourish; later, Pan Islamism replaced this with Saudi Arabia taking the lead. The Saudis emphasized the export of radical Wahabism as a foundational part of their foreign policy, which led to radical Wahabism taking on a life of its own. The Saudi's were effective in the export of radical religion and its ability to unify, but they did not expect the converts it produced to turn on them; the royal family expected Wahabism to legitimize them. That did not happen; it produced dissidents that looked beyond this life, and more importantly, it played a part producing bin Laden and others like him.

Bin Laden's radical version of Wahhabism owes no allegiance to any country, and this idea was used as a recruiting goldmine among multinational radicals and provided a common ground for a formerly divided terrorist networks. He first saw this in Afghanistan and capitalized on his accurate perception later. According to Bin Laden and others like him, Wahabism is the branch of Islam that most closely resembles the Salafis (first three generations of Muslims). Therefore they are not bound to a country, and they consider themselves harbingers of a new reformation that can only come about through the violent overthrow of existing regimes, and this view, unfortunately, resonates with a considerable number of

radicals. If they can continue to effectively transform this radical political movement into a conversion force for those with little or no religion (this is why he
targets the youth), America, its allies, and several Middle Eastern nations have
much to worry about. Bin Laden and others like him, will continue to gain emi-
nence in the eyes of their followers.

It is appropriate to look at the supranational force of this idea embodied most
noticeably in Bin Laden. As a youth he studied in Beirut and experienced first
hand the appeal of secularism, but rejected it due to his devout upbringing. During his backsliding days, while in his teens, he became a womanizer and heavy
drinker. His spiritual revival began when he built one of two mosques with his
father (Muhammad bin Laden, who was the leading contractor in Arabia by vir-
tue of his favor with the royal family) while simultaneously studying Islamic literature. His past experiences with Western influences caused him to cling more
tightly to his Wahabi heritage, and fear the seductive influences of the West. In
time he proved himself to others. He journeyed to Afghanistan in 1979 at the age
of 22 along with other youth who were motivated by a supranational call to
defend Islam in Afghanistan through the use of jihad. The result, he and many
troublesome youths would return to their homes radicalized.[37]

Troublesome youths showed up in New York, over 20 years removed from
Afghanistan, heavily influenced by Wahabism and other versions of Islam. When
these facts are coupled with the reality that 15 of the 19 highjackers were from or
had ties to Saudi Arabia, the evidence against this regime and what radical forms
of Wahhabism produce mounts considerably. In short, Wahhabism will prove
impossible to ignore and Saudi Arabia will have to bear the lion's share of the
guilt for its export.[38] The lion of terrorism was now roaring for jihad to continue,
and clearly linked to Saudi Arabia's tolerance and encouragement, but few took
note, and many underestimated the ability of those who participated in the
Afghanistan jihad.

**Previous assumptions leaned on the assertion that only radical regionalists
should be the targets of intelligence agencies. Those assumptions proved
faulty, because it underestimated the supranational appeal of radical Jihad.
It is obvious that both camps and their motivations need to be studied.**

The world has witnessed the effects of radical jihad on the desperate, poor,
uneducated people of Palestine and Central Asia as well as multimillionaires like
Bin Laden, the educated suicide bombers like Mohammad Atta, female college
students willing to blow themselves up, the Southern California preppie, and the

Hispanic former gang member, Jose Padilla, who was *"chillin"* in Afghanistan while allegedly learning how to build a dirty bomb. What if many discouraged inner city youth, college students, quirky adolescents, suicidal people, drug addicts and religious zealots found new versions of this faith appealing? What would happen to the streets of America if just a fraction of a percentage adopted the tactics of suicide bombings? It would be a mistake to underestimate the appeal of radical jihad, its tactics, and its effect on people.[39] The spread of rational irrationality should be a concern to every American citizen, and the dismissal of terrorists as mad men limited to geographical boundaries with a particular ethnic makeup, should soon go the way of other dinosauric theories.

First of all, in their minds, nationalists (those fighting for their homeland) and supranationalists (those fighting for their version of a universal Islamic ummah/community) are rational, and when their motivations and military limitations are considered, it makes sense for them to use suicide bombings as a tactic. Ehud Spitznak penned these words in October 2000 when he recalled the nationalistic suicide operation in Lebanon.

> "October 23, 1983, was one of the most horrific days in the history of modern terrorism. Two massive explosions destroyed the barracks of the U.S. and French contingents of the multinational peacekeeping force in Beirut, Lebanon, killing 241 American servicemen and 58 French paratroopers. Both explosions were carried out by Muslim extremists who drove to the heart of the target area and detonated bombs with no intention of escaping. Subsequent suicide attacks against Israeli and U.S. targets in Lebanon and Kuwait made it clear that a new type of killing had entered the repertoire of modern terrorism: a suicide operation in which the success of the attack depends on the death of the perpetrator."[40]

Suicide bombings shocked security experts on watch during Reagan's tenure. Shaken by this intrepid new irrationalism, they pulled out of Lebanon. Spitznak, the author of this piece, clearly stated that the only way to stop suicide attacks was to investigate their methods and motivations. Few American security experts listened to him then, but more are listening now. The fact that he and another Israeli, perhaps the world's leading voice on suicide terrorism, called for such research is not surprising given Israel's predicament over the last 20 years and their intimate knowledge of this form of terrorism. They cite several reasons that contribute to lethal minds carrying out marching orders in the form of suicide bombings.

Ariel Merari is the theorist Spitznak worked with and cited. Merari gave several reasons for suicidal operative's motivations. The findings are useful, but one must keep in mind the interviews are limited to Palestinians and Lebanese who fight for regional reasons, similar to the Kamikazes in WWII. After interviewing over 50 would-be bombers, Merari came to the conclusion that there is no single psychological factor in the individuals who chooses to participate. He states that the task of recruiters is not so much to instill the desire to take one's life in young men but to find people who are willing to do this and then reinforce it. Further, he claims that no organization can make a young person do this, but it can exploit their hatred of the enemy, incite religious beliefs, and exploit a profound sense of victimization in an effort to reinforce the desire for martyrdom.[41] The practice of propaganda that prepares the youth for martyrdom operations has been socialized into the minds of the youth, and now indoctrination can work. Palestinian terrorists know it. However, Merari has omitted in this article the fact that most of Palestine is saturated in a terrorist culture where the youth seek martyrdom or at the very least revere martyrs.[42]

Although suicide operations were always viewed as irrational and nationalistic in origin, the author asserts that radical versions of Islam are evolving into a supranational force. For the better part of the 60s and 70s nationalistic motivations could sufficiently explain most jihad activity, but supranational movements began to take root and occur right under the nose of the US during Afghanistan. Nationalistic interpretations of jihad remain satisfactory for some countries in the Middle East, Northern Africa, and Central Asia, and the use of suicide operations remain foundational due to the lack of military capability, but the transformation from regional to supranational terrorist organization can occur rapidly and may happen in Lebanon and Palestine if Hezbollah and several Palestinian terrorist groups choose to cooperate locally with supranational organizations.

Lebanon's political struggle continues with several factions vying for preeminence, and the result is political instability in this nation while Palestinians earnestly desire statehood. Iran seized the opportunity when it could and trained terrorist units to move in and used the banner of regional jihad. Iran instituted Hezbollah to attack its three favorite targets: America, Israel and Syria. Palestinians desire the elusive goal of statehood. By attacking Israel's sense of security through suicide operations, Palestinians hope to create a sense of helplessness on the part of Israeli citizens.[43] They hope this will force Israel to negotiate for peace and vote in politicians who are more sympathetic to the Palestinian cause. Awad Awad is a first generation American Palestinian who knows first hand that the struggles of his people are not a religious supranational struggle but a regional one. Awad understands his people's struggle and does not agree with America's approach to the Israeli/Palestinian conflict and offered this conclusion.

> "The term shaheed is only used in the Quran on a few occasions, and it refers to someone who was killed in the service of Allah. It was clearly used sparingly and seldom, because the prophet knew of many who died in battles, but he did not call all of them shaheeds. He only spoke of those slain in the service of Allah as being with Him. Shaheed was reserved for a select few. This term has been distorted in an effort to mobilize the people around an idea that will give them a state. But I think the only solution for that region is a two state region that is gradually integrated into a one state nation."[44]

Awad's articulation of the problem of radicalization is on target and calls for an end to the religious propaganda in Palestine and for both sides to own up to the injustices they have committed. Such honest and candid approaches on the part of the Palestinians and Israelis will prove more productive in Palestine. The problems that exist in Lebanon may grow worse due to the lack of American involvement and the entrenchment of a radical version of Shia ideas that consider violence an appropriate "surgical operation that a person should use..."[45]

Upholding Universal Shariah Law and the Lawless Ones

The contradiction between lawless actions and the desire for law is perplexing, but these radicals are not short on verses from the Quran and Hadiths to justify their actions. This new movement was formed against the background of fighting a titan during the jihad in Afghanistan, and each victory gave the Mujahideen new confidence. They believed that David, armed with shariah, could defeat a Goliath anywhere, and they gathered to discuss this belief in the mountains of Central Asia.

Author Robert Kaplan witnessed this firsthand and cites the desire of the Mujahideen for pure and unadulterated Islam as the primary reason for the supranational appeal of the Afghanistan Jihad. The Mujahideen that he lived with during his coverage of Afghanistan's war with the Soviet Union spoke often and frequently concerning their beliefs and their desire to see a return to the glory days of Islam.[46] Kaplan witnessed first hand the radical elements gaining a foothold in Afghanistan, but considered this a secondary issue. He admits to being "...caught up in the struggle to liberate Afghanistan, and my lack of objectivity shows." In retrospect he stated, "I just basically missed the phenomenon of Wahabis, Saudi extremists, joining the *Mujahideen*. It was a relatively small number of people, and because of that I assumed they weren't that important. It turned out they were."[47]

The author is uniquely qualified to speak to the issue of the supranational threat of Islam, because he was there during its infancy stages when no one else wanted to take the financial and health risks associated with such journalism. Robert Kaplan, Robert Bunker and Martin vanCreveld are part of a growing body of scholars who see the emergence of lawlessness and failed states as one of the biggest problems the international community will have to face in the future, and terrorism is a byproduct of this.[48] These authors are on the cutting edge of research into strategic forecasting, and they continue to emphasize supranational movements that render the state less effective. One of the foundations for this new lawlessness is based on religion. The terror strikes of September 11 released by non-state actors spawned in Afghanistan as well the other places mentioned in this paper, reveal that states no longer have a monopoly on warfare and lethality, but this author still believes the state will be the primary actor in warfare in spite of terrorism's ascent in warfare.

Western Bias of warfare claims that material goods are the primary reason that people fight. Historically, since the Treaty of Westphalia brought about the birth of the modern state, the emphasis of states has been their survival and their progress materially. But Islam, like any religion, is a supranational force that can be, and is, interpreted differently by individuals. As a revival in the interpretation of jihad as a duty catches on, pockets of youth will rise up and make statements through violence by attacking high and low value targets. The problem lies in the interpretation of jihad and how it is used to recruit people to a cause, especially those who believe their respective nations have failed them. People look for a cause, and as long as that search remains in the human heart, someone will seek to exploit it.[49] One need not look further than Central Asia to see failed states at work.

Central Asia is a haven for failed states and supranational yearnings. This trend in developing, and Third world countries will undoubtedly continue, giving rise to increased lawlessness and all forms of terrorism. Martin vanCreveld articulated this problem in his essay, "The Fate of the State."

> The State, which since the Treaty of Westphalia (1648) has been the most important and most characteristic of all modern institutions, is dying. Wherever we look, existing states are either combining into larger communities or falling apart; wherever we look, organizations that are not states are taking their place. On the international level, we are moving away from a system of separate, sovereign, states toward less distinct, more hierarchical, and in many

ways more complex structures. Inside their borders, it seems that many states will soon no longer be able to protect the political, military, economic, social, and cultural life of their citizens. These developments may lead to upheavals as profound as those that took humanity out of the Middle Ages and into the Modern World. Whether the direction of change is desirable, as some hope, or undesirable, as others fear, remains to be seen.[50]

This assessment is on target, and the Grim Reaper does appear to be hovering above several states in Islamic countries, particularly the Middle East and the 5 Central Asian former Soviet republic states: Uzbekistan, Tajikistan, Turkmenistan, Kazakhstan and Kyrgystan. Uzbekistan is one of the latest states to fall victim to this evolving form of radical Islam and this trend will undoubtedly continue.[51] Bin Laden and his Al Qaeda leadership will also undoubtedly continue to try and capitalize on this trend and stoke the embers of lawlessness in the hearts and minds of radicals.

Usamah bin Laden has consistently tried to manipulate this trend since the early 90s, and with each attack he has grown in stature. He has successfully tapped into Arab and Islamic anger and resentment towards the US. He is drawing from both camps of nationalism and supranationalism and has cooperated or merged with several terrorist organizations on logistics and training. He is aiming at unifying the youth who are the same age he was when he started his jihad over twenty-five years ago, and he is the leading voice of supranational jihad movements. He is bolder than ever.

Usamah bin Laden's Statements

August 96: Declaration of War
Our youths believe in paradise after death. They believe that taking part in fighting will not bring their day nearer; and staying behind will not postpone their day either. Exalted be to Allah who said:{And a soul will not die but with the permission of Allah, the term is fixed} (Aal Imraan; 3:145). Our youths believe in the saying of the Messenger of Allah (Allah's Blessings and Salutations may be on him): "O boy, I teach a few words; guard (guard the cause of, keep the commandments of) Allah, then He guards you, guard (the cause of) Allah, then He will be with you; if you ask (for your need) ask Allah, if you seek assistance seek Allah's; and know definitely that if the Whole World gathered to (bestow) profit on you they will not profit you except with what was determined for you by Allah, and if they gathered to harm you they will not harm you except with what has been determined for you by Allah; Pen lifted, papers dried, it is fixed, nothing in these truths can be changed "Saheeh Al-

Jame' As-Sagheer. Our youths took note of the meaning of the poetic verse: "if death is a predetermined must, then it is a shame to die cowardly"[52]

February 1998: Taken from bin Laden Fatwa "Jihad Against the Jews and Crusaders"

"All these crimes and sins committed by the Americans are a clear declaration of war on God, his messenger, and Muslims. And ulema have throughout Islamic history unanimously agreed that the jihad is an individual duty if the enemy destroys the Muslim countries. This was revealed by Imam Bin-Qadamah in "Al-Mughni," Imam al-Kisa'-in "Al-Bada'foreign," al-Qurtubi in his interpretation, and the shaykh of al-Islam in his books, where he said: "As for the fighting to repulse [an enemy], it is aimed at defending sanctity and religion, and it is a duty as agreed [by the ulema]. Nothing is more sacred than belief except repulsing an enemy who is attacking religion and life.""

On that basis, and in compliance with God's order, we issue the following fatwa to all Muslims:

The ruling to kill the Americans and their allies—civilians and military—is an individual duty for every Muslim who can do it in any country in which it is possible to do it [EMPHASIS ADDED], in order to liberate the al-Aqsa Mosque and the holy mosque [Mecca] from their grip, and in order for their armies to move out of all the lands of Islam, defeated and unable to threaten any Muslim. This is in accordance with the words of Almighty God, "and fight the pagans all together as they fight you all together," and "fight them until there is no more tumult or oppression, and there prevail justice and faith in God."[53]

December 2001:

"My beloved brothers in Islam,
Assalamu-alaikum wa Rahmatullahi wa Barakatuh
We have been struggling right from our youth; we sacrificed our homes, families and all the luxuries of this worldly life in the path of Allah (we ask Allah to accept our efforts). In our youth, we fought with and defeated the (former) USSR (with the help of Allah), a world super power at the time, and now we are fighting the USA. We have never let the Muslim Ummah down.
We should realize that this life is temporary and eventually we have to return to Allah (SWT), the lord of the Heavens and the earth.

The Jihad (fighting in the way of Allah) has become Fard-Ain (obligatory) upon each and every Muslim. We advise the Muslim youth not to fall victim to the words of some scholars who are misleading the Ummah by stating that

Jihad is still Fard-Kifayah. The time has come when all the Muslims of the world, especially the youth, should unite and soar against Kufr and continue Jihad till these forces are crushed to nought, all the anti-Islamic forces are wiped off from the face of this Earth and Islam takes over the whole world and all the other false religions."[54]

The following statements reveal not only the aim of Bin Laden but also his success in recruiting followers. Due to the fact that this is not a tit for tat approach to warfare, Bin Laden's confidence grows even when he at worst is faced with a life of hardship and deprivations, or at best, what he ultimately desires, martyrdom or a caliphate that he approves. No matter how successful Bin Laden is, he knows neither he nor anyone close to him, will ever live to actually rule over an Islamic regime. He has calculated the crown of martyrdom and his memory/ legacy in the Islamic world to be of far more weight than any temporal position of authority. Those who believe he actually wants to rule are sadly mistaken; his life will remain in the shadows, and he will opt for a legacy of martyrdom, which is consistent with what he has maintained all along.[55] His statements from a video found in Qandahar, Afghanistan also reveal his continued, persistent aim to convert the youth to his Islamic vision.

"Those youth who conducted the operations did not accept any fiqh in the popular terms, but they accepted the fiqh that the prophet Muhammad brought. Those young men (…inaudible…) said in deeds, in New York and Washington, speeches that overshadowed all other speeches made everywhere else in the world. The speeches are understood by both Arabs and non Arabs-even the Chinese. It is above all the media said. Some of them said what followed the operation were more than the people who had accepted Islam in the last eleven years. I heard someone on Islamic radio who owns a school in America say we don't have time to keep up with the demands of those who are asking about Islamic books to learn about Islam. This even made the public think more (about true Islam) which benefited Islam greatly.[56]

The fact that Islam is the world's fastest growing religion is indisputable and common knowledge. As it continues to grow, bin Laden is banking on radicalizing as many new converts as possible and linking jihad with his version of Islam. But orthodox Muslims must be heard as well so that they can clearly separate bin Laden's converts from the truly faithful. Bin Laden clearly interprets the rise in the numbers of converts to Islam to be consistent with his September 11 attacks and a jihad theology.[57] Omar Hazim believes that the growth reflects a message of the religion's true beauty and has nothing to do with jihad. He cites negative propaganda and a smear campaign by the West, and members of other faiths, as backfiring. It backfired in his opinion, because people without previous exposure to Islam are now curious about the faith. "They examine it, perhaps for the wrong reasons and in doing so they find it is not anything like its enemies have portrayed it."[58] The rise of Islam means that both the numbers of radicals and orthodox are growing and this should be a cause for concern.

It is clear that we need Muslims of good will on our side and the majority of Muslims are devout in their faith and their contributions to society are documented and well appreciated. As a representative of the faith of Islam, Imam Hazim has seen the face of the religion during his Hajj (pilgrimage to Mecca). Millions of Muslims have swarmed around the Kabbah and bore witness that "There is no God but Allah and Muhammad is his Messenger." It is here where race, class, education and citizenship are reportedly erased. "Religion can provide the blue print for the way people and nations interact with one another. Jihad is fought most perfectly within and not externally. Most Sunni, Sufi and Shiite factions agree to this. This is what we teach about Jihad in Islam. The Palestinian struggle and suicide bombings are an act of desperation, not a jihad. Al Qaeda members are criminals, not Muslims and our religion loves peace, not war."[59] Perhaps he and others can provide some spiritual containment for this radical version by continuing to disown and bastardize it.

And perhaps the struggle or jihad that is now taking place within the religion of Islam is a greater jihad for the religion itself, a jihad of the pen and tongue that can indoctrinate and socialize the next generation. The struggle for inward purity and righteousness is a fierce struggle for all Muslims. It calls all members to resist the temptation for violence, lust for vengeance, and primal lesser appetites inspired by what they believe to be the lower creatures, the jihn (creatures that tempts men to do evil deeds).[60] This struggle is ongoing, and the next generation of Muslims will determine the face of their religion and the culture their faith produces. They will also determine the regional and international security issues that accompany their interpretation of jihad. The idea of radical supranational jihad is no small matter, and the cancer is spreading.

Conclusion

September 11…was a day that forced the US and the world to face the awful truth about supranational terrorism and the lethal minds behind these attacks. The Bush administration took every effort to try and unmask the hidden face of terrorism and launched a media campaign against Al Qaeda.[61] Those who were more seasoned in the administration began to caution Bush about the length of this campaign and warned him not to single out a single man or group because this war was a long way from over, and it would continue far into the foreseeable future. America cannot soften its stand on terrorism now or in the future. Tolerance is not an option, and rational irrationalists will push our security experts to new levels of stress and frustration.[62]

This war will include the best efforts of military personnel, policy makers, civilian analysts and intelligence agencies, but will this be enough? That question and the task at hand for America and those who are on the frontlines of this war will remain for some time. America must learn from its enemies and understand their strengths and weaknesses. Propaganda and resocialization programs that will strike at the heart of radical jihad must match the ideas we are fighting.[63] Those who participate in terrorism must find the consequences unbearable, and the families of terrorists must not be rewarded for their participation in these acts. The new lethal minds must have the help of organizations that support and nurture terrorism in order to succeed, and the organizational reach of these movements and their tactics have unfortunately achieved the status of permanence in warfare.[64]

This paper is written with the hope of educating some members in public service who may be in a unique position to do something about the new face of warfare that will strike again on our soil in the future. Our enemy will simply never stop trying to harm us. They will not fight a tit for tat battle. They will attack us for their own reasons and purposes and raise their children to do the same.[65] America must prepare like never before, because every place we gather in numbers could become a potential target. Those who attack America will not relent and terrorists take courage in this fact by preaching to their converts the Quranic mandate to fight and never flee the battlefield, which is a grave sin in the Quran (Quran 8:16).[66] Since this is true we can confidently say that our enemies are ready, but are we? That said, the author offers this paper to those who are dedicated to fighting for and defending the treasure that is America. We must win this war and we can. To say we cannot is to admit defeat. Concerning victory friends, there are no obstacles left, only excuses.

Notes

1. Hazim, Hakim, Middle Eastern Interpretations of Jihad and the Far-reaching consequences" (Graduate Paper Unpublished) June 2002

2. Gharb is a territory of the strange, forbidden and dark. The sun sets here and all manner of fearful terrifying activities take place. It is symbolic and has been used to represent the Western world and its influences. (Mernissi, Fatima, author of first coin this term and lectured on this from her Morocco. She also uses this in her book...*Islam and Democracy: Fear of a Modern World.*

3. Bodanski, Yosseph, *Bin Laden: The Man Who Declared War on America,* (Prima Publishing 3875 Atherton Road, Rocklin CA) pp. 13–49

4. Salmi, Majul, Tanham, *Islam and Conflict Resolution,* (University Press of America Inc., 1998) pp. 122–25

5. Quran 2:198 (Note all Versions are the Yusuf Ali Translation)

6. Salmi, Majul, Tanham: Taken entirely from, *Islam and Conflict Resolution,* pp. 123–124

7. Usamah Bin Laden "Jihad is an individual duty" http://www.islaam.org.auarticles/15/LADIN.HTM August 3, 2001

8. Salmi, Majul, Tanham, *Islam and Conflict Resolution,* pp. 57–58 and Azzam publications "Seven Misconceptions In Fighting The Apostate Regime, <66.96.205.195/~azzam/html/articleshome.htm.n.d> date accessed August 2001. The general consensus of Shiites is that Jihad is an obligatory duty for all Muslims. They also the minority and regard Ali as the only true caliph and themselves as the true adherents of the faith. This is a rigid stance placing them at odds with the dominant Islamic population who are Sunni.

9. "Islam and Islamic History in the Middle East In Arabia and The Middle East", Islam City, http://www.islam.org/Mosque/ihame/Sec3.htm accessed 6/29/02, 5:37

10. Quran 2:256

11.Author unknown (Placed this introduction at the beginning of Imam Abdullah Azzam, "Join the Caravan" Exact date uncertain) <http://www.so.uc.edu/org/msa/mssn/joinaahtml>

12. Ibid. This was taken directly from Azzam's work Join the Caravan. It outlines the primary reasons for jihad and attacks the complacency of so many Muslims who fail to appreciate the nature of jihad and it becoming fard (obligatory) for every Muslim in certain circumstances.

13. Williams, Daniel, "Suicide Bombers Nurtured by Despair" "Washington Post" 2002

14. Cook, David, "Suicide Attacks or Martyrdom Operations in Contemporary Jihad Literature" (Rice University, Fall 2001)

15. Ibid

16. Burns, John, F., "Martyrdom the Promise that Slays Peace", New York Times Week in Review, April 2001

17. Hoffman, Bruce "Inside Terrorism" (Columbia University Press, 1998)

18. Barber, Ben, "Pakistan's Jihad Factories", (The World and I online Issue Volume 16, Issue 12) December 2001, page 72 < http://www.worldandi. com/public/2001/December/jihad.html>

19. Ibid

20. Ibid

21. Jessica Stern, "Pakistan's Jihad Culture" (Foreign Affairs (November/December 2000,Volume 79, Number 6)

22. Ibid

23. Shayk Ibn Jibreen Kayfa Nu'aalij Waaqi'unaa al-Aleem, (Worship Jihad, 10/27/2000) Note: Internet site no longer available document restricted to LEOs, Public Safety, Military personnel

24. Ibid

25. Bunker, Robert, and Hazim, Hakim, *Foreign Opfor Reader Occasional Paper3: Radical Islam and Al Qaeda Doctrine*, (NLECT-CW, LA, California, Feb. 2002)

26. Holy Bible, Micah 6:8 (NIV Version)

27. Azzam, Abdullah, "Join the Caravan"

28. Quote taken from Interview with (Akbar not real name) who requested not to be identified due to the fact his Father will not be allowed to come back to the US

29. Interviews with Akbar

30. N.B. Note abbreviation stands for New Beginnings. Interviewee lived in was born and raised in Lebanon number of years here was not disclosed

31. N.B.

32. Rashid Ahmed, *Jihad: The Rise of Militant Islam in Central Asia* (Yale University Press, 2002) pp. 223–24

33. Ibid

34. R. Freeman, Interview, 1978, Summer

35. Muhammad (Alias: Fard) Source did not want to give any more information

36. Mike Tolbert, Interview, March 11, 97 (Mr. Tolbert resides in Topeka, Kansas and is a 20 year veteran of the Armed Forces. He is Currently a captain at Shawnee County Correctional Facility.

37. Bodanski, Yosseph, Bin Laden: The man Who Declared War on America pp. 1–25

38. Hazim, Hakim, "A Declaration of Jihad", TEWG Seminar, January 2002,

39. Ibid

40. Spritznak, Ehud, **Rational Fanatics** (This article was originally published in the September/October 2000 issue of *Foreign Policy*.)

41.Ibid. Note: Ariel Merari Tel Aviv University psychologist. The author disagrees with some of Mr. Merari's assumptions particularly about the nature of forcing one to be a suicide bomber because that is obvious and his argument does not sufficiently address suicide operations outside of Palestine. Indoctrination and not poverty and victimization produced a mindset that is willing to commit martyrdom operations in the World Trade Center attacks. There may be more of a willingness to commit these acts in a group context than a solo operation but culture produces such people and creates the desire for such a reward by offering this option much in the same way that all activities that are considered legitimate in a culture draw a number of people to them. These people are then encouraged to pursue their interest.

42. N.B., AKA New Beginnings, Note: Source is formerly from Lebanon and well acquainted with Hezbollah and the PLO

43. Hamas Strategies and doctrines and Charter, <http://wwwariga.com/treaties/hamas.htm> Accessed August 11, 2001

44. Awad, Awad, Interviewed, March 20, 2002 Note: Awad is a first generation American Palestinian who is also a National Security Studies student at Cal State University San Bernardino

45. Ayatollah Muhammad Hussein Fadl Allah [sic], "Islam and Violence in Political Reality", "Middle East Insight, Vol. 4, #4 and 5, 1986, pp. 4–13
Note: Taken from the secondary source:Alexander, Yonah, *Middle East Terrorism: Current Threats and Future Prospects,* (G.K. Hall and Co., An Imprint of Macmillan Publishing Co. 886 third Ave. East Suite NY, NY, 1994) p. 50

46. Kaplan, Robert, Interviewed by Katie Bacon "The Atlantic Online", "Atlantic Unbound", Nov. 2, 2001 http://www.theatlantic.com/unbound/interviews/int2001-11-02.htm

47. Ibid

48. Bunker Robert, Interview via Email July 5, 2002

49. Hazim, Hakim, "A Declaration of Jihad" Seminar, Long Beach State University, April 14, 2001

50. Van Creveld, Martin The Fate of the State© 1996 Martin van Creveld From *Parameters*, Spring 1996, pp. 4–18.

51. Roy Oliver "Changing Patterns Among Islamic Movements", Brown Journal of World Affairs (Winter/Spring) 1997

52. Usamah bin Laden "Declaration of War" 8/23/96 http://msanews.mynet/MSA.NEWS

53. Usamah bin Laden "Jihad Against Jews and Crusaders World Islamic Front Statement" February, 23, 1998

54. Usama Bin Laden, KANDAHAR (Islam News): Daily news, articles and interviews on the Jihad in Afghanistan <http://www.azzam.com>

55. Hazim, Hakim, "A Declaration of Jihad", TEWG Seminar, January 2002,

56. bin Laden, Usamah, Transcript of Video Tape, [Translate by US government officials and Dr. Kassem M. Wahhba] Made public 12/13/01, found on numerous websites.

57. Ibid

58. Omar Hazim, Interviewed by telephone at his residence in Topeka Ks, May 18th 2002 [Omar Hazim is an Imam of quite some standing in the Mid West area and he has been associated with Islam for 39 years. He is a published author and has lectured in several Mosques in the US. He was selected by his peers to address a congregation of 7000 after the end of Ramada, the Islamic month of prayer and fasting]

59. Ibid.

60. Ibid.

61. President George Bush, Associated Press care of MSNBC Breaking News, September 11, 2002

62. Spritznak, Ehud, "**Rational Fanatics**" (This article was originally published in the September/October 2000 issue of *Foreign Policy*.)

63. Bunker Robert, Interview via Email July 5, 2002

64. Spritznak, Ehud, "**Rational Fanatics**"

65. Hazim, Hakim, "A Declaration of Jihad" Seminar, Long Beach State University, April 14, 2001

66. Cook, David, "Suicide Attacks or Martyrdom Operations in Contemporary Jihad Literature" (Rice University, Fall 2001)

Virus: Al Qaeda and Infectious Militant Cults

By Hakim Hazim

October 2002

Definition of Sects and Cults: *Sects begin when a leader emerges with a different message than the orthodoxy and separates himself and his group from the original body or doctrine. However, the sect still retains some of the foundation of its original doctrine while cults resemble little of the original faith and alter or interpret texts randomly in order to suit their own aims and claim a place of special revelation or authority from God. Cults are characterized by extreme devotion to the leadership as the embodiment of God's will or a supreme idea. Whether secular or religious, the group is willing to make supreme sacrifices.*

Definition of Militant Cult: *A militant cult is any religious or idea based group that teaches, practices, trains or encourages their followers to use violence in ways other than self-defense against others as a legitimate way of obtaining favor with God or furthering a supreme cause. Militant cults are derivatives from major religions or idea based systems. They are threats to regional, national and international security.*

Militant Cult Theory

My theory states that militant cults have five features:

1. **They are derivatives of major religions or idea based systems and not acknowledged as legitimate by the larger body.**

2. **They use violence on civilians and security forces in order to obtain favor with God or advance an idea. God or the idea is perceived as inevitably triumphant.**

3. **They have a charismatic leader who demands total devotion to his will, and the individual losses his sense of self in the group.**

4. **Recruitment and indoctrination of others are ongoing efforts.**

5. **Violent acts that likely lead to death of self in an attempt to harm others are exalted as a desirable end and valid expression of faith in God or an idea.**

The virus of militant cults will remain due to four reasons:

1. **The irreversible position of most cult leaders and members render negotiation and diplomacy ineffective or useless.**

2. **Failing states and regime states are breeding grounds that provide a significant supply of radicals.**

3.   **Due to the success of suicide operations some hostile states will choose asymmetric battle plans against America in the future, and this will give rise to more sponsors of terrorism in which the manufacture of militant cults motivated by religious beliefs or ideas are but the latest weapons in the arsenals of nations.**

4.   **Individuals who are dissatisfied in their nations will resort to violence against it as a means of expression and communication. Other militant cults & sects through leaderless resistance may inspire them as well.**

"A person who is guided by God's will, will never be misguided by anyone, and a person who is misguided by God can never be guided by anyone." Usamah bin Laden (Usamah bin Laden often opens his speeches with this Sunni proverb)

Al Qaeda and other militant cults cannot be deceived; they are rightly guided, and God has commanded every action they have undertaken. Cults of this type seek to worship God by using violence against unbelievers and advancing His causes in this way. It is frightening to know this is the entire reason for their genesis. Yet make no mistake, Al Qaeda and other militant cults are nothing new; they had simply never achieved such remarkable success until September the 11th. Since that date, they have come into full public view, and what is worse, it's only the beginning. A cult, by strict definition, is a radical derivative of any religion that has been altered to the point where it is no longer similar to the original version it claims to adhere to. Cults are therefore shunned by the larger body of believers, and develop an "us against the world" mentality. Worldliness in all forms, (which to a degree is normal) is strongly rebuked and gradually purged away until all attachments are broken, even the attachment to life itself. Exacting sacrifices are imposed upon devotees, and it is often unbearable for most, causing many to leave; yet, even as the demands sift their numbers, it increases the commitment of those who choose to remain. By marshalling the ability to stare death in the face, and welcome it as a reward, members are able to give a limitless commitment, a characteristic that separates them from other soldiers.

   Militant cults and their cadres of suicide bombers had previously been viewed as mentally deranged members of fanatical sects, similar to deranged cult members here in the US. In the US, Messianic Christian cults were familiar. They faced their deaths as well, but did not seek to take members outside their group with them. Two familiar cases featured the Jim Jones' cult and David Koresh's Branch Davidians. Both were land-based militants who were preparing for the end of the world, and in preparation, murdered government agents (congressman and ATF officers) whom they believed were facilitating Armageddon. Both groups did themselves in, to the heartbreak of many bereaved family members. California's own Heaven's Gate cult followed this pattern of indoctrination and simply committed mass suicide, disappearing with the passing of a comet. As they faced death, it was enough for them to lose only *their* life, but Al Qaeda and groups like it, want to harm others in the process of terminating themselves. In fact, this is the reason the suicide action is undertaken.

Experts in the fields of psychology and sociology have also concluded that Al Qaeda and similar groups are cults, and this is based on extensive research into this phenomenon. Margaret Singer, an emeritus professor of psychology at California Berkeley University, simplifies a cult's method of control by listing and outlining what she has named the 5 Ds: deceit, dependency, debilitation, dread and desensitization.

> Converting new members has little to do with the content of a cult's teaching and everything to do with control of information to silence critical thinking, experts say. Margaret Singer speaks of "the five D's"—deceit, dependency, debilitation, dread and desensitization—by which cult members are recruited and transformed. "It's a step-at-a-time seduction, so the person hardly notices they are being changed," says Singer, an emeritus professor of psychology at the University of California at Berkeley. According to Singer, the recruitment of the Sept. 11 suicide pilots almost certainly began with "the first D"—deceit. Our campus is loaded with Middle East people, and talking politics is about the central thing they like to do," Singer says. "So some guy can recruit into his terrorist organization by saying, 'Come on over to my place tonight and meet my friends, and we'll talk politics.'
>
> Almost certainly, she says, Mohamed Atta was not approached by someone asking him, "'Say, how'd you like to commit suicide?'" As part of the indoctrination, cults try to isolate prospects from family and friends who might give alternative opinions. Simple techniques such as sleep deprivation, or psychological or even physical abuse, help reduce resistance to the cult message. Presented often as "consciousness raising," an opposite process actually occurs. The gradual constriction of thoughts and awareness begins to create a cult personality, paving the way for the second and third "D's"—dependence and debilitation. The new member hears and sees only what the cult leaders approve. Communication with the outside is cut off. To reinforce the member's group identity, a new name and distinctive clothing may be provided. The fourth "D"—dread—comes from fear of the cosmic punishment that members think they would suffer if they offended the cult's leaders. Desensitization—the fifth "D"—grows naturally out of an us against them attitude. By

accepting that the cult is good and the rest of the world is evil, cult members have no guilt about their actions." Taken from Long, James "Cults, terrorist groups share chilling similarities, experts say" The Oregonian/November 9, 2001

Al Qaeda is no ordinary cult; it's an evolving entity and an idea that seeks a base; that is what Al Qaeda means, the base. They are seeking a base within Islamic populations who are willing to convert to their ideas. Al Qaeda answers the question of what happens when a cult evolves into a movement with military discipline and training. The answer is this, a widely popular movement in some areas of the globe that will win support from disciples, radicals and state actors intent on harming their enemies. Even those that do not agree with its creeds will lend their support because of its military usefulness. Tempting, Al Qaeda is for those who hate America. It is an ally intent on pursuing America and its interests to the ends of the earth. Al Qaeda is a militant cult that hits and runs, disperses and incorporates into the population around it. "The Base" is committed to generational warfare, and it indoctrinates it members in such a way that they are able to live amongst the enemy, taste their pleasures and remain fixed on an objective that was laid out years ago.[1] This cult possesses a zealous brand of faith, and generational warfare is not uncommon; its members view the present battle as but one chapter in the struggle between believer and unbeliever that God has ordained, a struggle God has promised believers the victory in. Perpetual jihad is both a virus and a WMD, worldview maintained by deception. It's a virus that is transmitted from mind to mind by skilled and convinced indoctrinators whose mission is to win the hearts of a younger generation of Muslims.

The problem of threat assessment that the US is currently trying to solve now is more troublesome than any threat assessment challenge previously faced, because of the various factors involved in identifying the threat. Previously, declared and undeclared enemies always fell into the category of nation-states. Now, not only are there the traditional enemies of nation states, there are also the nontraditional, shadowy, nonstate, transnational entities that are being manufactured outside of and within America's borders. Terrorists could be used as delivery systems of WMDs by hostile states or their own leaders. This has caused the US to change military strategy and opt for preemption towards nations they believe harbor terrorists—-a sharp break from the policy of massive retaliation.[2]

Numerous terrorists are currently undergoing training as of this writing. A Nigerian native recently spoke these chilling words to the author about military cults. "Hakim they (America) don't get it; it's not an Arab thing. People in *my* country love bin Laden. He has given them money and kind words. They consider him very pious and devout. Not only do many Muslim Nigerians love bin Laden but some have joined Al Qaeda and some women are dedicating their *unborn* babies for service in jihad."[3] Experts have kept a close eye on many terrorist activities in predominantly Arab and Central Asian countries, but they have underestimated the reach of radical military cults and their ideas in places like the former USSR, Africa, and many parts in the West, including US soil. And this is the very reason the maxim of Sun Tzu becomes more relevant. "Know your enemy." Troublesome and perplexing is the lack of understanding concerning the ideology behind the movements of radical military cults that use Islam as a cover for their actions. Studies in the area of an enemy's ideology were very useful during the Cold War, and America was filled with numerous experts on communism. Our military forces are highly trained and are determined to defend our interests wherever we send them, but this will become an increasingly difficult task when friend and foe cannot be distinguished in foreign lands, and every military victory will only add to the flames of hatred if a diplomatic push and socialization programs are not coupled with such actions.

America is not dealing with Special Forces; it is dealing with the birth of militant cult forces propagated by Al Qaeda and others. Cult members understand that there is no room for doubt, and they are duty bound to follow their leaders into battle. Exceptional converts become cell leaders and the imam for the groups, and their primary responsibility is to interpret the scriptures in military terms. Here is an example of a cell leader's control over his group's actions. These are the words of the world's most famous highjacker, Mohammad Atta.

> You must not show any signs of nervousness or stress and be joyful, happy, cheerful and calm because you are about to carry out an action that Allah loves and that pleases him. Then there will follow the day when with Allah's permission you will be with the nymphs in paradise, accordingly smile in the face of adversity young man for you are departing to the eternal paradise.[4]

Contrast this mission statement with the recollections of a childhood friend and this becomes vexing to the mind. "Mohamed, I remember him, completely in a form of child...innocent, virgin, smiling and laughing and feeling with life...He likes life. He's a very delicate person" His friend also made this statement.

> Oh, of course. I knew him before we got into the faculty. He was a very helpful man, and friendly. So friendly. So that all of us, or maybe the majority, not all to be much more accurate, the majority of us tending to take him as a

friend, a close friend to tell him some secrets about themselves or something like that. And I have never found him annoying or something, or feeling that he don't want to share with people's pain or something. He was very helpful. He was a very good listening person. And he was completely polite. Polite with the complete meaning of this word, really. His raising up, as I knew was surrounding with the most basics of morals. His father, looked after him so much. He has only one sister, and his father is a very, very gentle and moral person. "[5]

The appeal of radicalization and the cult following some clerics receive should not be underestimated. Youth, like Atta, who find themselves searching for answers in the spiritual realm may best be described by the Apostle Paul who stated in 1st Corinthians 13, "for now we see dimly…" and in another place, Acts 17:27, "…that they would seek God, if perhaps they might grope for Him and find Him, though He is not far from each one of us." In this state, many strange things appeal to a seeker looking for God, and if orthodox religion does not have an appeal, radicalism will speak for God and offer guarantees that orthodox branches cannot. A cult can spring up anywhere there is a young seeker and radical versions of the faith are taught. Atta (and others like him) was seeking and groping in a dim, dark place until the beauty of jihad was revealed to him and suddenly there was a purpose to his life. The following Quranic verse was no doubt quoted to him, "Fighting is prescribed for you and you may dislike it, but it may be you dislike a thing that is good for you and love a thing that is bad for you. And Allah knows and you know not." (Quran, Surah 2:216) This passage is often cited by terrorists and taken out of context by radicals like Atta. They give their followers a choice between two options, heaven or hell. Jihad, they say, is the only guarantee of an entrance to paradise. Atta looked after his cell. He preached, assured, guided and kept his members on course until they reached their targets. He told them they were members of a new force of men, chosen by God to strike at the Goliath of their day. In Atta's mind, Allah intended jihad to continue until the Day of Judgment. Armed with a revived truth that set him and the other members of his cell apart, they bonded more tightly, and grew cynical and hostile towards the world around them. The vice-like grip of conviction secured their hearts and will until the day they crashed into the psyche of America and the world forever. Two Goliath like symbols came crashing to the ground.

Endless Jihad: The Perpetual Struggle

According to some Islamic traditions, this ongoing war between East and West is a part of prophecy and eschatology (study of end time beliefs). Muhammad's statements in the Quran and Hadiths spoke of the ages to come, and what would befall many Muslims. For many Muslims, not just radicals, it would be blasphemous to not believe the prophet. The majority of Muslims believe in the prophecies of Muhammad and these prophecies contain many Last Days scenarios that could be used to convince believers that they are living in the end times. For military cults, there is no better place to be. Dr. Timothy Furnish has published several papers on Mahdism and eschatology in Islam, and he believes that Mahdism and eschatology will play an important role in politics and religion in the future. Further, he believes that bin Laden could claim the title of Mahdi for himself.

> Throughout Islamic history many religio-political leaders have claimed Mahdi-hood. Most rapidly faded back into obscurity. Some gathered followers, however, and a few took power. The most successful such movements were the Abbasids in the 8th-century CE Islamic heartlands, the Fatimids in 10th-century CE Egypt, the Almohads in 12th-century CE North Africa and, most recently, Muhammad Ahmad's followers in the 1880s in Sudan. Several other Mahdist-type movements in the last two centuries succeeded by transforming into separate religions: the Baha'is of 19th-century Iran, the Ahmadis of 19th-century India. In recent years only two such movements have developed in the Middle East: that of a self-styled Mahdi in Saudi Arabia in 1979, which met with a violent end; and the *sub rosa* movement that accompanied the success of the Ayatolloah Khomeini, in which whisperings that he was the Mahdi (Hidden Imam to Shi[c]ites) went undenied.[6]

The author of this paper corresponded with him by email and does not believe that bin Laden will claim such a title, but agrees that eschatology is playing a role in the Islamic world today. In the future, eschatology will become even more viable.[7] Consider the widely held beliefs of most Sunnis and Shiites. Many Muslims believe that a rightly guided caliph will emerge at the end of the age and bring about a change in the disparity between Muslim lands and apostate lands.[8] Radical groups and cults that emerge often speak of instituting their version of shariah law, which will be the foundation all Islamic regimes. Most Muslims believe that when orthodox shariah law is implemented and faithfully practiced, Allah will grant the ummah (community of believers) victory over their enemies. The logic flows this way, no shariah, no caliphate (rightful successors to Muhammad and leaders of the great community of believers) no Caliphate, no al Mahdi, the promised deliverer of Muslims everywhere who will emerge from the newly instituted Caliphate. Most Muslims believe that a revival of the ummah will come from spiritual awakening due to divinely inspired scholar's pens, but militant cults have opted for the violent overthrow of existing regimes. After this overthrow, Islam will then be imposed on all subjects. The entire thrust and aim of most radical organizations is the removal of unjust rulers and Western influence, followed by the establishment of shariah, and the eschatological expectation of a caliphate. Where does this eschatological yearning come? They originate in the Quran and some of the Hadiths (Sayings of the Prophets). Muhammad told his followers this.

> "Prophethood (meaning himself) will remain with you for as long as Allah wills it to remain, then Allah will raise it up wherever he wills to raise it up. Afterwards, there will be a Caliphate that follows the guidance of Prophethood remaining with you for as long as Allah wills it to remain. Then, He will raise it up whenever He wills to raise it up. Afterwards, there will be a reign of violently oppressive [The reign of Muslim kings who are partially unjust] rule and it will remain with you for as long as Allah wills it to remain. Then, there will be a reign of tyrannical rule and it will remain for as long as Allah wills it to remain. Then, Allah will raise it up whenever He wills to raise it up. Then, there will be a Caliphate that follows the guidance of Prophethood." [9]

For the purpose of simplicity, the 5 stages that Muslims (who regard these Hadiths as authentic) believe in are:

1. The Reign of the Prophet Muhammad
2. The Caliphate: This period includes the first four or Rightly Guided Caliphs. It was a Caliphate that most Sunni Muslims believed followed the rules according to the guidance revealed to the Messenger of Allah. This period is called the reign of the rightly guided Caliphs: Abu Bakr, Umar, Uthman and ending with the murder of Ali. This generation is also known as the Salafi.
3. Lesser Apostasy: This reign contains some injustice to a varying degree between one king and another. This period started after Al-Hasan bin Ali and includes the Umayyad, Abbasid, Mamluks and until the fall of the Ottoman State in the twentieth century. This period includes all states that ruled in the Muslim world during those centuries.
4. Greater Apostasy: the reign of the tyrannical rule: This period started around the end of the Ottoman state and continues. This reign includes all the regimes that ruled the Muslim World since that date.
5. The return of a Caliphate: Is a prophecy that points to the Last Days and a time when the Caliphate is reinstituted. Allah is once again pleased with Muslim lands, and in response to this, He will send a rightly guided caliph, al Mahdi, to lead Muslims in a series of military victories over unbelievers and apostate regimes. [10]

Muhammad listed five stages of Islam in his hadiths. According to many scholars, when believers stray from the faith, especially leaders, it withdraws the blessing of Allah from them and weakens the Ummah. Some Muslims are waiting for a revival. The awakening will come through the scholar or the martyr, and each member of the Ummah must decide for itself. The violence adherents are not winning yet, but they are gaining an audience. The expectation for something better furthers the conviction that they are in the age of the greater apostasy. This message strikes a chord with the masses, and since there are no relevant competing ideologies, a new version of Islam emerges, and one that calls its adherents to take action, violently. Adherents of this new version must reject their leaders, and tell their followers to do the same. Immediately, they begin radicalizing their members and forming a sect. If this continues and they are ardent enough, they will become a militant cult that seeks to establish a pure Islamic nation. The majority of all radicals say the same thing, "We want a pure Islamic state." How will that be accomplished? Blood must be shed. Abdullah Azzam has outlined the way to success for all nations. He died in Afghanistan fighting a Jihad in a failed state, Afghanistan; his tale is told today through his blood and ink.

> History does not write its lines except with blood. Glory does not build its loft edifice except with skulls; honor and respect cannot be established except on a foundation of cripples and corpses. Empires, distinguished peoples, states and societies cannot be established except with examples. Indeed those who think that they can change reality, or change societies, without blood, sacrifices and invalids, without pure, innocent souls, then they do not understand the essence of this Deen and they do not know the method of the best of the Messengers (may Allah bless him and grant him peace).[11]

Militant Cult Leaders in Regime States: Contemporary and Historical Figures

Militant cults often find a home in regime states, and these nations are prevalent in: Central Asia, Northern Africa and the Middle East. A regime state is defined as a group of ruling elites in undemocratic, third world countries who rule over their populations as dictators. Most of these elites have one primary pursuit as their aim, remaining in power. This often results in harsh crackdowns towards any political opposition or dissention. Machiavellian politics reigns in these countries, these regimes claim to be Muslims, but their open hypocrisy breeds contempt, and the only other acceptable political alternative for its citizens is radical Islam. Militant cults are a virus that can easily find homes in regime states that care very little about their populations. Why do people convert in the crucible of failed states? Because the majority of these populations are facing a miserable existence when both their nations and this life offer them little hope, and the only thing that sparks them is the afterlife or empowerment in this life; this version of Islam offers both. It also gives an opportunity to the successful youth to become heroes. Citizens react in a normal way to oppression; they look for leaders who will fight for them. Eventually leaders emerge, and the motivations simply don't matter. Whether one fights for nationalism, Pan-Islam or the clan is irrelevant; they fight because that is the only way to change things. Keep in mind the participants are receiving something from this fight, respect, weapons, food and most importantly a faith that promises eternity for their participation.

One need not look further than Uzbekistan to find the perfect example of an opposition leader, Juma Numangi, and an oppressor, the leader of the former Soviet republic, Islam Karimov. Many resent Karimov for the following reasons: tyranny, his heavy-handed approach to Islamic opposition groups, extending his presidency, and an overall secular approach towards governing.[12] Dictators like Karimov will always find people willing to overthrow them, and those opposing these regimes will be able to turn the people's passions against these tyrants. Once this occurs, Clausewitz third side of the triangle, the passion of the people, will come into play. Radical Islam calls its people to action, and one's conversion to it means he is a soldier.[13] Passion must be directed towards a target and this is where Clausewitz trinity is still effective. The latent passions of the people are awakened, and this is what every charismatic leader is able to do. By guiding the passions of the people towards a particular target, the leaders of these movements will be viewed as God's agents to implement a shariah based state. This is still a Clausewitzian trinity but with a twist.[14] Juma Numangi was a young Charismatic leader who faced the east for the first time when he witnessed the courage of the young Mujahideen in Afghanistan, and he was the founder of the Islamic Movement in Uzbekistan. Numangi decided to do what a militant cult leader does; remove the apostate, but in order to that he must win the support of the people. He formed IMU in order to accomplish this.

The Islamic Movement of Uzbekistan, or IMU, is regarded as a destabilizing factor in Central Asia. Numangi's popularity has soared in the last three years due to Karimov's tyrannical approach. Karimov is a holdover from the old Soviet regime and confronts problems the same way the Soviets did, violently. From the perspective of his enemies, he is fighting God's will, and he is viewed as an apostate headed for the fire. Currently he receives support from the US while simultaneously oppressing his people. Human rights groups routinely publish his crimes against his people. The US, to its credit, has made an issue of the abuses, but it is too little, too late. A military cult has taken root in Uzbekistan and is spreading to other parts of Central Asia. As it continues to spread, those who fight in jihad are viewed as the real heroes, none greater than Juma Numangi, who caught a glimpse of the glory of jihad years ago when he was in Afghanistan.[15]

Numangi was one of many young Central Asian conscripts who served in the USSR/Afghanistan conflict. He and his fellow soldiers returned home from the war with courageous tales of how brave the Mujihadeen soldiers were. He developed a profound respect for all of those he fought against. For a young Central Asian struggling with the idea of what to live for, anything that seemed to represent something meaningful would be appealing and he, like so many other young conscripts from this region, received an answer when he looked into the eyes of his enemies and beheld fierceness, loyalty and bravery.[16] In order to be a true soldier, Numangi would have to possess what they possessed, something he obviously lacked. The question was how?

The haunting of conscience began to drift into the mind of Numangi, and he and his fellow conscripts desired to emulate something grand, courageous, and eternal. Numangi and his followers began to question their motivations for living. They needed a deeper faith, one like the Wahhabis; this seemed to be the only alternative to their current life. How could they remain inactive and cowardly after they witnessed those mujahideen? The clan identity was not enough for them and ultimately they sought an identity that went beyond the shallowness of these ties. Political Islam in the form of a militant cult would give this to them. Numangi officially formed the Islamic Movement of Uzbekistan in 1998, and is still considered a mysterious cult like figure with the same aims as Al Qaeda and the Taliban. He has launched successful guerilla attacks against Karimov from Tajikistan and Afghanistan. Now that the US and Russia are vying for influence in this region, the IMU will certainly become more active.[17]

Numangi is the new cult leader, surrounded by mystery and intrigue, but this is the effect of this version of Islam. It creates the illusion of a caliph type with impeccable Islamic credentials, even when the leader clearly lacks them. Numangi's is not credited with being charismatic or with having a deep understanding of Islam, and a quote from a previous ally confirms this. "He is a good person but not a deep person or intellectual in any way, and he has been shaped by his own military and political experiences rather than Islamic ideology, but he hates the Uzbek government—that is what motivates him above all. In a way he is a leader by default because no other leader is willing to take such risks to oppose Karimov." [18] Uzbekistan is another failing state that has been affected by the radical movement born over 20 years ago in Afghanistan.

Sudan and the Mahdi of the Late 1800s

Turkey and Egypt ruled most of Sudan in the late 1800s, but these regime states met their match in the person of a mysterious Messianic figure. Muhammad Ahmad Abdallah was born on August 12, 1844. He was a deeply religious man who sought to teach other Muslims the faith. Mystical he was, belonging to the branch of Islam known as Sufism, and as a member he often received messages in dreams and visions.[19] He studied under Shaykh Ali Kannuna from 1861–68 and gained a reputation for extreme asceticism. After he left his master, he quickly gained a following of his own and soon became a master with disciples. Upon the death of his master he received Kannuna's disciples that were now spiritual orphans, and he became the leader of the Sammaniya order.[20] As his influence grew, so did the admiration of his disciples and whisperings concerning his place with Allah began to circulate among the followers. The climate of Sudan was ripe for revolt. Egypt and Turkey vexed the majority of the Sudanese population, and calls for armed resistance were common, but never amounted to any real threat for the occupiers. Religion was important, and the pious Sudanese looked to the heavens and asked for a deliverer who would rid them of the cruel apostates who had made them subjects to their whims. Teachings concerning the Mahdi were well known in Sudan, and the expectations grew as years of oppression continued.[21]

Muhammad Ahmad Abdallah became the deliverer, al Mahdi. The confirmation came to him in a vision in which he claimed the prophet Muhammad spoke to him. Allegedly, Muhammad told him during this encounter that he was the senior khalifa and the expected Mahdi, and all who doubted this were apostates destined for fire.[22] Buoyed by this new confidence, he informed his closest companions and began to plot a course whereby he could mobilize the people around his command, and expel the apostates. Religious fervor took hold of him, and he made a public announcement of his new revelation and what this meant for everyone who would follow him. The expected Mahdi had come, and the proof of his manifestation would be the blessings of Allah during his military campaigns.[23]

This Mahdi was given to fasting and made his home in a cave, so suffering and deprivation would not be something he feared, nor would he allow his followers to fear the oppressors. The Quranic statement, "Oppression is worse than death." was well known in Sudan's Islamic circles and often quoted to boost the spirits of those who took part in jihad. [24] Al Mahdi's preaching revived his followers with hope and renewed spiritual dedication. It also produced a slaughter of 1400 of the occupiers' soldiers, and this was the beginning of a militant cult that was zealous for God and blood.[25] The battle for Sudan continued, and in 1883 British Col. William Hicks led an army of 8000 Egyptians against the Mahdi, to his own annihilation. The effect? All of Sudan began to declare Abdallah the Mahdi. Tribes joined him in vast numbers, too many to arm, so with sticks and stones this army of zealots would rush out to face their enemies. At the height of his power he laid siege to Khartoum, and after 317 days his troops breached the defenses and massacred 40,000 people including the British General George Gordon. Five months after this stunning victory, the Mahdi died.[26]

The Mahdi died, but Mahdism did not, because his successor, Abdullahi, established the Mahdiya (Mahdist regime) as a way of keeping the movement alive.[27] The British had other thoughts about this movement, and the Battle of Omdurman in 1899 was the end of this militant cult that was then led by Abdullahi. Abdullahi and his force of converts met the fury of the Maxim gun. In spite of heavy losses, they persisted with cavalry charges. They continued to rush unflinchingly towards certain death, which for many of them meant an eternity in paradise.[28] The lesson is this, if a militant cult can influence all of Sudan and later take root with the Taliban, start a worldwide revival of a militant jihad movement, and grow roots in Uzbekistan, how far-reaching will this problem become in the future?

Conclusion: Realism's use of Suicidal Idealism

People say that our feeling is of resignation, but that does not know at all how we feel, and think of us as a fish about to be cooked. Young blood does flow in us. There are persons we love, we think of, and many unforgettable memories. However, with those, we cannot win the war. To let this beautiful Japan keep growing, to be released from the wicked hands of the Americans and British, and to build a 'freed Asia' was our goal from the Gakuto Shutsujin year before last; yet nothing has changed. The great day that we can directly be in contact with the battle is our day of happiness and at the same time, the memorial of our death. [29] Kamikaze suicide pilot

Japan's case was different; they manufactured cultic suicidal tendencies in their young men in order to use them as an extended arm of their military. They promised eternity to their young, and the young men were certain the Divine Wind would carry them home. The Japanese believed their emperor was a god incarnate, so the foundation for nationalism and religious fervor meshed perfectly in the nation. This is a perfect example of how states can create suicidal operatives. Non-state entities obviously can as well. The US faced this before. America is no longer idealistic about our enemies. Nations and non-state actors envy and hate the US and September 11 changed democracy forever. America is vulnerable, and virtually everyone in the field of national security has concluded that future attacks on US soil will yield greater lethality. The first approach to this battle was to go after the state actors that host terrorists. By meeting out unacceptable punishment to regimes that sponsor this type of warfare, the Bush administration hopes to send a clear message to any state that dares to sponsor this form of warfare. This is realism at work. The theory of realism names the nation-state as the principle actor in international affairs. Realism states that all nations seek enough power to maintain autonomy at a minimum; at a maximum they seek ways of extending their influence and power.[30] This is viewed as natural; therefore, one can realistically expect some of America's enemies to resort to this type of warfare in some form in future wars. What Afghanistan did may seem irrational, even unthinkable to most idealists, but Afghanistan was seeking a way to expand its influence and power in the Islamic world.

Most nations will remain rational, even when they use militant cults or suicide operatives. Four nations have made rational decisions to use militant cults, jihadists or suicide operatives to expand political influence or wage low intensity war in their respective regions, Afghanistan, Iran, Pakistan and Saudi Arabia. America funded the Mujihadeen in Afghanistan not realizing that many in that movement would water the seeds for militancy later. These nations used militant cults to further their causes; and for the most part, they were acting within the realm of realism and taking calculated risks. A summary of realism states:

1. The international community is basically anarchic and without any permanent law enforcer.

2. Nations choose to settle their scores through flexing their muscles and going to war when they deem it necessary.

3. Power is the key in this theory, and nations that possess economic and military power are able to glean most of the benefits from the international system.

4. All nations form alliances and coalitions as a way of balancing and dealing with more powerful nations. [31]

States sometimes form alliances with militant cults, jihadists or suicide operatives, and this becomes a form of balancing or securing military leverage. Asymmetric warfare in the form of terrorism is a rational choice for states when militant cults are readily available and expendable. America must prepare for this new weapon.

In contrast, idealism is still trumpeted by democratic peace theorists and those who believe that international law can be effective in the world community. Idealism came about due to the carnage of WW1, and gave rise to a fundamental change in the way nations viewed war. It was largely due to the immense popularity of Woodrow Wilson at the conclusion of the war and the revival of Immanuel Kant's philosophy.[32] Idealism was fueled by the shock of carnage after WWI. When this was coupled with the inhumanity of chemical weapons, few nations had the stomach left for war. These two were thought to be enough to change the way nations viewed conflict and the hope for an age of peace was trumpeted. Roughly 20 years later, an aggressor blitzed out of Europe and pulled the rest of the world into a war that produced weapons that could virtually end all forms of life on earth. Idealism should have ended here, it didn't.

Human nature did not change after WW1. Nations continued to seek out ways to maintain their autonomy and increase their power abroad, because it is the natural thing to do. Nations are comprised of human beings, so the same truths are applicable to them are true for groups, clans and transnational actors; human nature with all of his frailties and sins are constant wherever human beings gather. Militant cults are zealots who fight because they believe they will increase their possessions in the next life or leave a legacy to be admired behind. Fueled by these ideas, they are confronting nations and their civilian populations. Advancing their cause in the here and now is rational when viewed in this light.[33] Below are some examples of militant cults, jihadist or suicide operatives in the service of, sponsored by, or aided by a state:

1.   America and the Mujahideen in the Afghanistan/USSR war

2.   Iran and Hezbollah in Lebanon

3.   Japan and the Kamikaze pilots against the US

4.   Saudi Arabia's Madrasah inspired fighters located in Central Asia, Pakistan, Kashmir, Afghanistan and the Taliban & Al Qaeda jihadists.[34]

History tells us that this type of warfare will continue. America will be hit hard again. Brace for it; it is coming.

1. Hakim Hazim, Lethal Minds: Radical Jihad and the Creation of the Terrorist Mindset. (Occasionally distribution by author and National Law Enforcement and Corrections Technology Center-West upon request, October 2002)

2. The National Security Strategy of the United States of America, Released on September 20, 2002

3. Source lives in Southern California and will be returning to Nigeria in a matter of months

4. Professor Jerrold M. Post "A Mission to Die for" Washington, Monday 22 October 2001 Liz Jackson interviews Professor Jerrold Post, the Director of the Political Psychology Program at George Washington University. **http://www.abc.net.au/4corners/atta/interviews/** Aug. 29th 2002 2 PM

5. Mohamed Mokhtar El Rafei, "A Mission to die for" Washington Sunday October 14th, 2002 Liz Jackson interviews Mohamed Mokhtar El Rafei http://www.abc.net.au/4corners/atta/interviews/mukhtar.htm 9/21/02 434 PM

6. Furnish, Timothy, "Mahdism in the Sunni Arab World Today" Regional Issues: Middle East Jan/12/2000 www.isim.nl/newsletter/4/regional/12.html

7. *Furnish, Timothy, "Bin Laden: The Man Who Would be Mahdi", The Middle East Quarterly, Spring 2002,* http://www.meforum.org/article/159 *Sept 22, 2002, 2:37 AM*

8. *Ibid*

9. A. Hijazi, "Al-Mahdi, Muhammad ibn Abdullah and A Caliphate That Follows the Guidance of the Prophet sallallahu `alayhi wa sallam" 1995 http://www.witness-pioneer.org/vil/articles/aqeedah/al_mahdi.htm, *Sept. 22, 2002, 2:45 AM*

10. William Green: "Central Asian Politics" Lecture Series at Cal State University San Bernardino (Winter 2002)

11. *Azzam, Abdullah, "Martyrs: The Building Blocks of Nations" Azzam Publications, Dec. 2001* www.azzam.com *accessed Feb. 12, 2002*

12. Rashid, Ahmed *Jihad: The Rise of Militant Islam in Central Asia* (Yale University Press, 2002 pp. 3–6

13. 28.Mark T. Clark, "The Continuing Relevance of Clausewitz," *Strategic Review* (Winter 1998), 60.

14. *Hazim, Hakim, "The Hydra of Political Islam in Afghanistan and Uzbekistan" March, 2002 (Unpublished)*

15. Oleg Yakubov, "The Pack of wolves: The Blood Trail of Terror" (Moscow, Veche, 2000)

16. Ibid

17. Hakim Hazim, Lethal Minds: Radical Jihad and the Creation of the Terrorist Mindset. (Occasional Paper #5 National Law Enforcement and Corrections Technology Center-West, October 2002)
18. Holt, P.M., *The Mahdist State in Sudan 1881–1898: A Study of Its Origins, Development and Overthrow*, (Oxford At The Clarendon Press, 1958) pp. 45–47
19. Ibid
20. Shaked, Haim, *The Lfie of the Sudanese Mahdi*, (Transaction Books, New Brunswick, N.J.,1978) pp. 64–65
21. Ibid
22. Ibid
23. Mcdonald, W, Wesley, "Osamah Bin Laden's Forerunner" (The World and I Online) 2001
24. Ibid.
25. *Holy Quran*, Sura 2: 191.23
26. Mcdonald, W, Wesley, "Osamah Bin Laden's Forerunner" (The World and I Online) 2001
27. Ibid
28. Chiran Tokko Heiwa Kaikan (August 14, 1994)
29. Morganthau, Hans and Thompson, Thompson, Kenneth, W. "Politics Among Nations: The Struggle for Power and Peace"(McGraw Hill College Div Dec, 1985)
30. Ibid
31. The Avalon Project at Yale Law School: President Wilson's Fourteen Points, Jan. 8, 1918 < http://www.yale.edu/lawweb/ÿvalon/wilson14.htm>
32. Morganthau, Hans and Thompson, Thompson, Kenneth, W. "Politics Among Nations: The Struggle for Power and Peace"(McGraw Hill College Div Dec, 1985)
33. Hakim Hazim, Lethal Minds: Radical Jihad and the Creation of the Terrorist Mindset. (Distributed by Author and National Law Enforcement and Corrections Technology Center-West upon request, July 2002)
34. Ibid

Section II

LATENT THREATS:

RUSSIA'S HISTORICAL AGGRESSION

SHIISM IN IRAQ & IRAN

NORTH KOREA'S JUCHE IDEOLOGY

Latent threats in this book are defined as nations that could turn against the US and its allies. I have named them latent, because the nations obviously have not taken hostile, warlike actions against us yet. Nonetheless, the job of any watchman is to spot potential dangers and call attention to them. There are numerous authors who have sighted some of the concerns I have concerning Russia and the Iraq/Iran connection, namely Shiism, and North Korea. I have examined these countries because of the deeply invested interests the US now has in solving these problems. America has invested a great deal of aid in assisting Russia since the collapse of the Soviet Union and has hopes for them becoming a functional democracy. The US has also invested billions of dollars into operation Iraqi Freedom and the rebuilding of Iraq. Blood has been invested as well to the tune of hundreds of American and Iraqi lives. The largest number of casualties from the terrorist nexus emerging in Iraq belongs to Shiites, nearly 12,000 to date. Clearly democracy will have significant problems, and the question that must be answered is this, were these efforts aimed at creating a Shiite nation alongside of Iran? Less visible on my list of latent threats is North Korea. I cannot honestly write a book without mentioning the internal workings of North Korea. Not only does the Kim regime possess a large military with nuclear capability, the regime has successfully indoctrinated the majority of the nation; turning many into willing cannon fodder if they should be invaded. I will highlight North Korea last and use the eyes of a former political prisoner. Her words will prove haunting and more effective than my research.

America has found itself in a new position of friendship with both Russia and Iraq recently and every effort should be made to remain conciliatory, but it should not at the expense of compromising America's preeminence in world affairs. There are potentially destabilizing factors that may cause current foreign policy approaches to move grossly awry. Sociology teaches us that unique cultures create worldviews that guide them and their nations towards particular goals. Democracy is the product of Western culture, and many Western nations have championed the rights of the individual and have shaken off forms of government considered oppressive and tyrannical. The further East one moves, it becomes rather obvious that democratic reform and democratic peace theory will run into serious problems in these regions.

This does not mean that one should abandon hope of democratic reform and the expansion of democratic ideas into Eastern countries, but great care must accompany this approach, and the countries in question must bear a great deal of responsibility in making such changes. The US has trumpeted the spread of democracy as the canopy of its new foreign policy approach, but at the end of the day, is our nation credible in its statements, and is Iraq, Iran and Russia seeking democracy and the liberation of their citizens from previous tyrannical ideas and leadership, or are they using our aid to create new centers of power in their respective regions? (I maintain it is the latter.)

Russia & US/NATO Relations: The Past, Present & Future

Hakim Hazim

© *November 2002*

One thing is certain, US led NATO expansion marches on since its conception, and this will continue to happen...as surely as death and taxes. How Russia deals with the inevitable and the measures it introduces for leverage in Eastern Europe are causes for NATO concern and circumspectness. An analysis of what Russia's past actions have yielded diplomatically and militarily provide insight for their future interactions with the US/NATO nexus. [1] Under careful examination, the future can be forecasted with some reasonable assurance. Russia fears the growing influence of US led NATO policy anywhere and particularly its backyard, Eastern Europe. Russia's weakened economy, its diminished conventional military, and limited economic capabilities are saliently impressed upon the national psyche. These factors, coupled with the Chechen conflict, force Russia into bargaining from a position of weakness, something very uncomfortable, uncommon, and unacceptable in the eyes of the Russian leadership. [2] Russia will play ball, but this is a deceptive tool used only to buy time, while it seeks to return to superpower status and emerge as the nation it has always longed to be. Russia has lost its status as a superpower, and these painful reminders nest in the hearts of its leadership. Russia is historically and culturally a country that takes a long-term approach to acquiring its interests, whether militarily or diplomatically, and the US should use guarded skepticism in all of it interactions with Russia. [3]

Russia's Historical and Present Diplomatic Strategies

Russian cooperation with NATO reached a new high with the Russia/NATO Council in 97 (NATO-Russia Founding Act), but this did not raise the hopes of Eastern Europeans. The Majority of Eastern Europe states yearn for a move towards democracy, and they welcome the mechanisms that are in place to accelerate their entrance into NATO. The PFP, Partnership for Peace, is one such mechanism, and even though several Eastern Europe states joined early, their main concern was a newfound competition amongst its neighbors and a new race to join NATO. [4] Although most Eastern European countries agreed that entry into NATO and the European Union was desirable, their primary concern was the time frame it would take to make these goals a reality and how much influence Russia would be given in the decision making process. These nations were concerned about removing the stumbling blocks that hinder their ambitions to join NATO. The stumbling blocks are: lack of resources, lack of political sophistication in the form of democracy, and Western sensitivity to Russian displeasure. [5] Russian displeasure is often voiced through diplomatic channels and strategy.

Russia's diplomatic strategy has historically been opportunistic, persistent and skillful. In a post September 11 world, the opportunity has emerged again. There must be cooperation because the American/NATO nexus and Russia are desperately afraid of WMD proliferation. If Russia changed from a cooperative disposition and openly or clandestinely exported WMDs or the technology, NATO's fears certainly would increase exponentially. Because of these concerns, Russia now possesses an even greater voice in NATO. In fact, May 14th 2002 brought about the formation of a NATO/Russian Council. This was certainly a new milestone. It gave Russia a partnership position with NATO allies in matters of terrorism, arms control and international crisis management. Previously in 97, Russia attempted to cooperate more fully with NATO until the bombing of Yugoslavia stalled this cooperation and placed a wedge between the two.[6]

The pact with NATO in 97 reveals Russia's aims, which are essentially the same today. Sergev Pegov noted that Moscow set two main tasks before its diplomats in the process of negotiations with NATO in 97:

1. prevent an increase in military threats stemming from NATO enlargement

2. make Russia an equal partner in the process of shaping a new European security system. [7]

He believes that Moscow has succeeded in achieving both goals, albeit with some minor exceptions such as NATO reluctance to bind itself with a commitment to not deploy conventional armaments on the territory of new members. However, Russian success has not been uncommon in the realm of diplomacy, and its strategies are effective in negotiations with the West. [8] There is a historical precedent for such negotiations. Keep in mind negotiations with NATO are primarily negotiations with the US and the following paragraphs illustrate this.

Russia often relies on US tendencies towards unilateralism to forge an advantage in the court of public opinion. The guise of cooperation and concern for the safety of humanity was raised with the ABM and INF treaties and the most recent treaty in Moscow. In order to secure the INF treaty in December of 1987, the USSR cited its withdrawal from Afghanistan and their willingness to remove launch based weapons that were already produced and deployed. This was an attempt to remake their image in the court of international opinion, and paint America as an aggressor bent on acquiring weapons and delivery systems designed to produce greater lethality. [9] Although Russia clearly has a nuclear advantage, it consistently states it is only looking for parity and reduction of forces.

According to Russia, nuclear parity is the only means to world peace, and the US and other members of NATO are viewed as threats to that parity. They believe that a nuclear balance between Russia and the NATO alliance checks aggression and maintains peace. As recently as this year they were willing to cooperate with China as a means of securing a multipolar world and claimed that the abandonment of the ABM treaty would cause international instability and start a new arms race. Vladimir Putin claimed a unipolar world was unsafe. [10] Russia relentlessly attacked America's motives for scrapping the ABM treaty and pursuing a missile defense. The other voices in NATO were considered irrelevant, and Russia chose to focus on the US alone and ignore the other members of the alliance, *because their negotiations with NATO are clearly negotiations with the US.* The Russian pattern of negotiating includes the following:

1. Persistence toward a stated goal

2. Resistance toward US initiatives

3. Deception: arguments concerning the common good as a way of winning international support

4. Concession when Russia realizes it must yield

5. Forming a back up plan to continue their goal under a refurbished idea

Concession does not mean that the Russians have abandoned a particular pursuit because the pursuit is always maintained; it simply means they sought to buy as much time as possible while forming a back up plan to continue their stated goal after the concession. [11] Concerns about the ABM treaty have been raised by the Bush 1 and Clinton administrations, but nothing was officially done about them due to Russian resistance through diplomatic channels and the use of the international media. The negotiations between the US and USSR when they were both superpowers began roughly 34 years ago.

US/NATO & USSR Negotiations

In 1967 the US/Soviet Summit was initiated by the US and it proposed strict limits on anti-ballistic missile systems, and this was the beginning of other summits and treaties. The Soviets flatly rejected the initial strict limit proposal, but in 72 the Soviet position softened, and the ABM treaty became a reality. Negotiations became strained again in 1983. In 83 two things happened: the discovery of the Krasnoyarsk Radar system that was under construction and the concept of SDI (Strategic Defense Initiative). The Soviets clearly had no intention of abiding by ABM treaty it signed in 72, and SDI was conceived due to the deception of the Soviet Union. Unashamedly and unflinchingly, the Soviets demanded an end to SDI and attempted to try the US in the court of international opinion, something the US was clearly vulnerable to. To counter this, the US trumpeted the construction or the Krasnoyarsk system in the international media and pushed ahead with SDI. SDI's conception became the focus of innovative and defensive technological pursuits. This changed the way the US thought about warfare.[12] On October 23, 1989, the Soviets conceded that this was a violation and pledged to dismantle the radar. The following years produced an endless number of discussions and summits, due to the fact that the Soviets and their Russian successor continued to decline militarily, and had no desire to see the US prosper. [13]

US triumph in the Cold War over Russia has caused Russia to seek a way of retaining its advantage concerning nuclear weapons by insisting on adherence to the ABM treaty, a treaty that was clearly in favor of the Russians because it never dealt with reducing the weapons that were off limits. George W. Bush made his case for the abandonment of the treaty early on in his presidency, and once again it was the US that stood in the position of accused. [14] The Bush administration's strategy was careful and catered to Russia. It omitted Russia as a threat or reason for abandonment of the treaty and pointed the accusing finger towards "rogue nations." (This is exactly what the Russians wanted to hear and this allowed a remaking of their image in the international community) Eventually the *Bear* got what it wanted, a favorable treaty.

The US and Russia recently signed a treaty (Washington Treaty) of arms reduction that still needs to be ratified by the senate. As of this time, the treaty would reduce US warheads to the level of 2000–2500 down from 6000. It gives both countries the option for deep storage or disarmament. Since Russia does not have the financial ability to disarm the majority of its warheads, it will still place most of them in deep storage. This is no cause for celebration if one believes in deterrence. US should remain concerned over Russia's tactical or battlefield nukes believed to outnumber the US at least a 3 to 1 ratio by the most conservative estimates, and these remain outside the treaty's scope. In the final analysis of things, Russia still received a treaty that left them with the advantage in nuclear weapons. [16] The ABM treaty and Washington treaty are excellent examples of Russian strategic diplomacy with the US and NATO. One president was able to withstand this strategy, and turn the tables on the USSR, and his example should be studied.

Not only did Ronald Reagan aggressively pursue a policy of giving the military and NATO whatever they needed, but he also pressed the USSR to give up the arms race by conceiving the strategic checkmate of SDI. The thought alone terrified the USSR, and Gorbachev knew the US had the economic capability to pursue such a strategy. If the US remained persistent in the new race, it would break the economic back of the Soviet Union; therefore, the negotiations began. The Soviet Union began to thoroughly change in its approach to the West and sought a way of modeling its country, to some degree, after the US. During negotiations with the US, Gorbachev consistently brought up the issue of SDI, demanding that the US give this up. [17] In the eyes of the world, he became a leader of peace and a model for sensibility in a senseless arms race, but history reveals he was a desperate man who had to remake himself into something Western. Reagan dictated negotiations, and he borrowed his maxim from the Soviet position of bargaining and "Peace through strength," was a phrase he was fond of saying. The Soviets were forced to make concessions; this they understood; they resented it, but they understood that they had for all practical reasons, lost the Cold War. [18]

This again revealed the uniqueness of the Russian way of negotiating. First of all pressure is exerted squarely on the nation it deliberates with, and the nation must justify the necessity of their position. The nation's position is cross-examined continually, and if agreements remain in flux, Russia publicly accuses. The accusations continue until the other nation concedes certain things that the Russians desire. [19] By relentless attacks on the state's motives, they recast the nation into the image of aggressor. Although the Russians don't fool anyone, they are no peacemakers; they effectively tarnish the image of those they accuse. This pattern continues in times of war as well. When engaged against smaller countries, the same tactics remain in place. These tactics continued in Afghanistan and more recently in Chechnya. Chechnya, a break away republic in Russia, and Afghanistan became two enemies associated with human rights violations and terrorism according to the Russian (state owned) press. [20] In time, the real aggressor in both situations was revealed, and even though the Afghans and Chechens were no angels at the onset of and during conflicts, they were not the demons the Russian (state owned) press made them out to be. The military mindset that dominates the various leadership positions today is a mindset that believes that a strong military is the key to Russian renewal. Hence all negotiations serve that purpose. This is historically applicable as well. A brief look at the origins of the Russian military mindset and its continuation will add more light to what America can expect in the future from the latent threat of Russia.

The Russian Military Mindset

William Hyland had much to say in his paper, "NATO: The Next Generation" (Westview Press, 1984). The author's thesis asserts that the history of Russian expansionism and foreign policy dates back to Peter the Great's desire for parity with the West. Hyland writes about a "Russian national psychology" that will rally behind any czar figure if the masses believe that Mother Russia is in danger. This is confirmed by the historical record of the 19th century suffering that Russia has endured under WW1, the Bolshevik Revolution, WWII and Stalin's purges. These examples led the author to conclude this concerning the Russian people and leadership, "In defending Mother Russia, they have an unparalleled capacity for suffering." [21] With these things in mind, Russian concerns over NATO expansion in Eastern Europe are understandable when viewed from their mirror-imaging (the tendency to see others motives the same way as yours) perspective. In short, since it is equality or superiority with the US that Russia is seeking, the US must diminish. As the US and NATO grow economically and militarily, Russia diminishes. This is an inverse relationship and a zero-sum game that Russia is engaged in.

Tatiana Parkhalina asserts a particular thesis concerning Russian/NATO relations that should be reviewed by NATO partners. The author argues that NATO enlargement has emerged as the overriding factor in Russian foreign policy due to the notion that there is a national consensus against it. With these things in mind there are several factors at play in its strategy: As an issue the nation can rally around, NATO enlargement serves to shift the gaze away from Russia's real problems, which are primarily economic and lack of political viscous or identity. In fact, Russia's own interests would be better served through cooperative engagement with the main international institutions, including NATO, to meet the new challenges it faces, but that is not their way, nationalism is. [22] Russia is willing to show a pretense of cooperation in order to push through its own objective in the council.

Without a proper understanding of Russia's history, issues with American/ NATO & Russian cooperation remain cloudy and give rise to speculative answers that omit its reasons for asserting a resistance-based policy towards NATO expansion. Just what does Russia expect from NATO, and what would satisfy them? There is unprecedented cooperation between Russia and NATO at present, but will this continue? The new reasons for friendly terms rest on:

1. Russia's desire for a better economy

2. Declining military might

3. A desire to look progressive (Western)

4. The need for US/Russian cooperation during the recent War on Terrorism

5. An opportunity to have a say in the affairs of Eastern Europe

A look at some of the previous posturing may provide a balanced view and give the reader insight into the hard feelings that still linger between the US led entity known as North Atlantic Treaty Organization and Russia. Some of the reasons for these persistent feelings are: Memories of a Cold War that was lost, a Warsaw pact that did not endure and an ad hoc CIS that never lived up to any of its expectations. All of these fuel Russian resistance. In short, the Bear is wounded and picking its fights one at a time, for now, it's Chechnya. Allowing NATO expansion to move into Eastern Europe, particularly the Baltics sends a message that Russia does not pose a real threat in the minds of the NATO members, because of the new friendlier terms, due to NATO's preoccupation with terrorism. However this is a sharp break from the military doctrine of 1999 which reflected an aggressive policy of first strike use with nuclear weapons if Russia or its allies perceived a threat. That doctrine was strong evidence of the inverse relationship between declining conventional weapons and the reliance on nukes, the last remaining symbol of former military glory. [23] Russia is willing to be friends now and play partner and defender against terrorism while it deals with its internal problems.

> The prospect of NATO enlargement, which creates the greatest resistance and fear in Russia is the likelihood of membership for the following three Baltic states of Estonia, Latvia and Lithuania. If only one joins, it would bring NATO into former Soviet Union territory for the first time. [24]

The historical Soviet imprint of the military is locked in the psyche of Russians. Significance of the military and the role it played in Russian culture can be traced back to Peter the Great and more recently the Brezhnev doctrine that stated once a nation became Soviet it could never reverse course. [25] History was viewed as linear, progressive, and intentional even inevitable, and war was a natural consequence of oppression and necessary vehicle for change. War was not to be resisted, but embraced and rigorously prepared for. Russia has a resiliency cycle that has enabled them to bounce back from catastrophe after catastrophe. To part with such a strong tradition of military resiliency would be more than just a decision to change; it would not be Russian. There are nostalgic longings for military superiority that the communist party ushered in, now present in the holdovers within the Duma and political leadership. Communism was compatible with Russian culture and its approach to warfare and politics. The Soviet Union was a vehicle based on historical Russian policy. The loss of nationalism was fine as long as the Russians were able to redefine Russian nationalism into a new identity of a socialist man that was rejected by Germans and the West in general. [26]

Culture is the product of geography, history, ethnicity, and most importantly the ideas about what these things mean to a particular group and how those norms effect relations with outsiders. This is significant because what happens next is the defining of who they are versus who others are. This reality is reflected in the way Russia and NATO have engaged each other. NATO (Western progressiveness)) and Russia (Eastern backwardness) are continually at odds over expansion and the tit for tat approach to negotiations are clearly advantageous to Russia, because although NATO is in a position to do what it wants, at least for time being, the opportunity to reconcile with a former adversary is very tempting. The culture of Russia and its foundation of dominance and aggression against others seem to be ignored as evidenced by this NIDS 95 statement that pushes for further cooperation. While stating NATO should maintain its sovereignty, the statement is clearly aimed at appeasing the Bear and not appearing dominant.

> NATO-Russia relations should reflect Russia's significance in European security and be based on reciprocity, mutual respect and confidence, no "surprise" decisions by either side which could affect the interests of the other. This relationship can only flourish if it is rooted in strict compliance with international commitments and obligations, such as those under the UN Charter, the OSCE, including the Code of Conduct and the CFE Treaty, and full respect for the sovereignty of other independent states. NATO decisions, however, cannot be subject to any veto or droit de regard by a non-member state, nor can the Alliance be subordinated to another European security institution. [27]

The backwardness of Russian military culture raises legitimate concerns. These concerns are understandable, because Russia must look after their security, but there is a paranoia factor driving the military mindset. Russian history and communism previously built this into the minds of the leadership in order to make conscription a right of passage for its citizens. The inevitable challenge of preparing for war, specifically nuclear, was something every citizen was familiar with, and this reality followed him or her like a shadow, reminding them of the seriousness of their struggle. Communism forced the community to share in everything, not just the goods of society but also the duties. If one shares in the fruit he must also share in the labor, even the terrible labor of war. Nuclear war was after all winnable and inevitable according to Soviet thought. Capitalistic aggression would initiate this conflict. These concerns still linger when Russia views the US and considers the limits of cooperation. [28] Tatiana Parkhalina pens these words about Russian/Nato Relations in, "Of myths and illusions: Russian perceptions of NATO enlargement,"

> In general, the question of NATO enlargement has spawned many myths and illusions which are skillfully exploited by Russian politicians. For many Russians, especially those of the older generation, the problem of interaction with the West is above all psychological. It is heavily influenced by the Russian cultural tradition. Over the past three centuries, each time Russia confronted the fact that it was lagging behind the West technologically, social tensions ensued. The recognition of the gap was seen as proof of the need to draw on the West's achievements to modernize the Russian economy, but simultaneously Russia has always feared the negative influence of Western values on society and culture, which limited the scope for cooperation. [29]

Vestiges of the military mind-set have made a nest in the minds of the leadership in Moscow over the past 40 years. It is a worldview that calls for a readiness and willingness to defend Russian sovereignty no matter the cost. It is a mind-set that is distrusting of every neighbor it has, a mind-set that came up with the Warsaw Pact to keep nations who joined from leaving. The Soviets cleverly constructed the Brezhnev doctrine under the guise of ideology, and this was simply a way of justifying violence against breakaway republics that asserted their limited sovereignty. Domestic problems were settled by force and international solutions followed the same approach. This mind-set, is endemically Russian and characterized by readiness and willingness to defend itself against a massive invasion from innumerable enemies. Although Russia has not played on the paranoia factor much since September 11, its military doctrine has been updated and the boisterous talk of nuclear weapons is a striking feature that has been highlighted since 1993. [30] Not only does Russia's unique geography cause it to be vigilant, vestiges of it's previous Marxist philosophy linger still, fueling the paranoia even after the disintegration of the once powerful USSR.

The Cold War: Its End and a New Era for Russia and the US

To understand any movement one must understand its origins and its purpose. At the conclusion of WWII both East and West were split into, and the world began to fall into one of those two categories. Communism aggressively pursued ties with Second and Third-world countries and continued to rally behind the slogan, "Workers of the world unite." The US aggressively pursued European allies who were economically and militarily stronger than their Eastern neighbors and this policy left many of these countries at the mercy of the USSR. [31] This approach emboldened the USSR.

The USSR became a juggernaut that swallowed up smaller countries and whipped up anti-capitalism sentiment wherever its sole treaded. They armed some of these countries and placed military bases in Eastern Europe and Central Asia in particular. These populations were poor, undemocratic and in search of something. They became satellite countries for Soviet policy and were given the false sense of republic autonomy or limited sovereignty. The former Eastern European countries are in a current identity crisis. Wealth possession, capitalism and democracy are but an experiment and for many, a distant dream. The presence of communism in Eastern Europe was like a dysfunctional/abusive relationship between the husband and wife; the abuser was protecting them from capitalism, the way an abusive husband tells his wife he's protecting her from the outside world. We against them became code words for the inseparable nature of communism. The hammer and sickle became the symbol for all workers, and the Eastern European countries sacrificed any dream of progress for the manufactured identity their conquerors handed to them. [33]

Russia tends to view its rule in Eastern Europe in a more favorable light than its former satellites. Indeed, their faith had been shaken by the various powers that ruled over them, and the foundation of their identity remains in question. A parade of conquerors had their way with Eastern Europe, and communism seemed to offer the promise of brotherhood. communism promised equality for its entire population, and this was appealing to Eastern Europeans. This became a link to something strangely resembling parity with other nations, something they had not had access to since the great medieval kingdoms of Poland, Bohemia, Hungary, Wallachia, Serbia, and Bulgaria. Eastern Europe recalled this time and ignored the negatives, because they were accustomed to being a downtrodden, conquered people. Communism promised a sense of freedom, even dignity, in the face of Western Europe's obvious and stated superiority. [34] Now the West is here, offering opportunities communism could not, but Russia is still there guarding its interests.

The prophet Isaiah asked a question, "Does the leopard change its spots or the Ethiopian his Skin?" (The Bible, Jeremiah 13:23) Russia is a leopard. The guise of friendliness is just that. Both countries have clear policies when it comes to their aims in Eastern Europe. The US has a clear policy of dominance in all spheres, economic, militarily and otherwise. This is clearly presented in speeches and stated to allies and foes alike. In keeping with the policy of domination and intervention Russia shows its true colors as well and especially in Central Asia. Intervention is spelled out in Russia's Near Abroad Policy. Near Abroad simply means that when Russia believes that its security or vital interests are threatened it has the right to intervene in any manner it deems appropriate. There are a few things to mention here:

1. Russia actively stirs things up in regions that are unstable or too stable so that it can intervene

2. Russia seeks to keep the international community out of these interventions and acts unilaterally,

3. The interventions are usually always in countries that were formerly under their control [34]

With these things in mind, America must continue to expect such interventions in the future from Russia and remain sagacious even while it continues its path of self-interest through limited cooperation.

Russia's Near Abroad Approach

Is there unprecedented cooperation between the US and Russia? Some argue the precedent has been here before in 97. [35] Will this cooperation continue into the foreseeable future, and does this newly formed partnership serve the interests of both countries? Obviously Russia is cooperating, because it has accepted the fact that it cannot compete militarily and economically with the US. It remains in conflict with Chechnya, a conflict that it must win. Russia has resources within its borders and in Central Asia that it needs to export but is not in a position to do so yet, and last of all, it wants to keep influence in both Central Asia and Eastern Europe, and it cannot do this using the Soviet methods of division, oppression and exploitation. [36] It must appear European in order to continue near abroad approaches, and it must use a different vehicle, thus the guise of cooperation and diplomacy with the West. The NRC may help Russia in this regard.

The NRC (NATO Russian Council) was recently enacted to give Russia a greater voice in the affairs of NATO; however, a poll of 1,500 Russians published in the daily newspaper Izvestia May 15th confirmed that the Russian view of NATO and the US has not changed. Nearly half viewed NATO as a military organization that seeks global dominance, and more importantly, only 25% of the people that voted were viewed as pro-Western thought that NATO and Russia had common security goals. The poll was an accurate description of Russia's continued opposition to NATO plans to offer membership to 10 Eastern European candidates, including the area in the Baltics: Estonia, Lithuania, and Latvia. Former military chief, Wesley Clark added a more realistic American perspective, "There's always been resistance in Russia to aligning with the West." Adding that no one really believes Russia will take NATO expansion, "lying down" [37] The NRC will give Russia a peaceful way of asserting its influence in NATO.

An interesting point was raised in a recent article, and the question posed centered on a how the USA and Russia's new cooperation could limit the role of other NATO countries. This is what Russia wants and is after. The logic follows this process, if NATO's primary concern was always Russia, than the need for NATO may diminish when the US and Russia forge stronger ties, even an alliance. If Russia successfully remakes itself into an image of friend of the West and a partner of the US while relying on America's tendency to use a unilateralist approach, its strategy of remaking itself will work in its favor. Peaceful coexistence with the US until it finds time to rebuild itself for the third time in less than a century is a perfect strategy.

Russia has given in to the demands of the United States and NATO on several occasions. Poland, Hungary and the Czech Republic joined NATO in 1999 and this concession still smarts. But something worse will in fact probably occur next, the admission of the Baltic States to NATO. There is no love lost between Russia and the Baltics. Keep in mind the three Baltic States: Lithuania, Latvia and Estonia. Keep in mind two dates: January 1991 and 1940 when the Soviet Army forcibly incorporated the Baltic states into the empire.[38] We see Russia using the diplomatic approach in the form of treaties designed to benefit them. In March of 2001, Mr. Putin invited Mr. Adamkus to the Kremlin for their first meeting, which turned out to be a long and intense negotiation in which Russia pressed for a treaty guaranteeing Moscow's right to resupply its military forces in Kaliningrad—mainly with fuel—along this rail line. Eventually Russia had to relinquish its demands. [39] This pattern of recent concession has continued and does not appear to have any let up, and here are some examples of its recent acquiesce to US pressure:

> It has massively reduced its own global intelligence capability by closing the Lourdes listening station in Cuba and announcing its withdrawal from Cam Ranh Bay in Vietnam. Putin has put meaningful union with hard-line Belarus on hold, and he has not generated substantial pressure over NATO expansion. The president also has acceded to a U.S. military presence in Central Asia, and he reportedly will allow Russian oil companies to participate in U.S.-sponsored pipeline schemes. On the surface, at least, the rewards for these concessions have not been evident. To the contrary, the United States has taken a series of steps that are clearly not in Russia's interest. For instance, by January 2002, it was apparent that the United States was developing a long-term presence in Central Asia. Russia had believed that the U.S. presence in the region would be temporary and based on strategic understandings that were trilateral—including Russia in the bilateral relationship with the host country[40]

Near abroad takes its roots in a policy that suits the Russian approach to peace making and peace creation. It mirrors Stalin's policy of fearing stability or competence in regions that are independent. Nations that are progressive are able to form alliances with other nations, and counter the influences of stronger ones. Russia fears the independence of any of its former Soviet satellites because it not only would mean a potential new adversary, but it could mean a rival for resources and influence. [41] One could rename this policy "Until we get or act together no one will." In fairness to the Russians, security issues remain because when neighbors and former allies are weak, they cannot threaten you (militarily or economically). The prospects of Eastern Europe countries threatening Russia are not likely, but the prospect of satellite countries with NATO bases restraining its movements are serious issues to consider.

The Soviet Union's policies may have been an extension of historical Russian foreign policy. The inherent distrust of outsiders was birthed in Russia's geographical location and the fact that enemies surrounded it. Geographical vulnerability gave rise to an aggressive approach that caused it to actively conscript its population and seek military superiority. [42] This led to a series of campaigns from before the Time of Troubles to the Bolshevik revolution. Virtually all of these conflicts were born out of what Russia claims was the desire to maintain its security and make peace with its neighbors. The overwhelming consensus of historians is that virtually all of Russia's wars were aggressive and offensive in nature. This history can arguably give rise to a mirror imaging that skews the way Russian leadership looks at power and NATO.[43]

The US and its NATO allies are fundamentally different than Russia, a difference noted by Eastern Europe and the international community. Democracy is the feature that differentiates. Eastern Europeans remain in a state of caution and fear concerning their Russian neighbor. Russia is concerned about the Baltic States but is restraining itself in light of the new cooperation. Eastern Europeans desire inclusion with Europe and its various organizations, particularly the EU and NATO. When given a choice concerning partnership, they have and will continue to choose the West. Eventually the Bear will slumber no more. Russia will change its position on several foreign policy issues if it fails to achieve its end, which is greater influence in Eastern Europe. Russia has called Ukraine's desire to be a part of NATO a mistake and reminded them that their economy depends on Russian resources. [44]

Near Abroad policies of Russia remain rooted in its desire to subject its neighbors and retain influence. The divide and conquer mentality was evident in Stalin's nationalization language policies in Central Asia. It is again evident in the idea of peace making versus peace keeping, manifesting itself in forceful subjection of those who disagree. The Russian intolerance of dissent has caused them to prohibit public demonstrations in the past by dispersing gatherings with live ammunition. [44] It is also apparent that Russia did not acquire its views overnight. Culture is also the product of a particular geographical history, so there must be sufficient coverage of its military history and the mind-set that has been handed down. Many of Russia's hardline communist within the Duma and Politburo stubbornly cling to their view of the rest of the world and their resistance to integration. Russians once looked to their czars as "the gatherers of Russian soil and hardliners remain stuck in that mindset." [45] Whether soil or influence, the pursuit remains the same and resistance to this mentality on the part of NATO is required to check this latent ambition. Russia will not accept a secondary position to the US for long. It will seek ways and means to regain preeminence in international affairs; in order to do this the Bear must rebuild its military and serious problems remain in this arena.

Fading Military Might at the End of the Cold War

Russia's military has degenerated to a level that it is no longer formidable conventionally since the end of the Cold War. The struggle in Chechnya is well known, and the Russians are willing to employ whatever means necessary to put this breakaway republic in check. The obvious missteps of the Russian military in Afghanistan and Chechnya have yielded discouraging consequences conventionally. The military continues to struggle, and this proves difficult to swallow when the Cold War vestiges remain fixed in the collective mind of the top brass and politburo. Kindly, NATO refuses to mention the Cold War in terms of loss, favoring the fable that cooperation between Gorbachev and Reagan ended it, and future relations with the former superpower are but a continuation of these policies. [46]

However, the truth is the new cooperation that the US and NATO claim to have with Russia may be due to the war on terrorism and the need to secure the international community from terrorism, but it is basically opportunism for both nations. The US has embarked on a policy of pacifying Russia and highlighting mutual threats. Underestimating Russia's wounded pride would be a grave mistake on the part of NATO. Russia and NATO are not allies. We respect them because it would be easier to build a less hostile relationship with them than it would be to go to war. The proliferation of WMDs by Russia is a greater concern than ever since September 11. George Tenet specifically stated in April that the proliferation of weapons of Mass destruction was Russia's policy, and the US has demanded an end to this. Putin and his leadership must make a decision. A STRATFOR article highlighted this.

> This represents the beginning of a severe crisis between the United States and Russia. Putin must weigh his choices very carefully. If he accepts U.S. demands and subordinates Russian foreign policy to Washington again, he acknowledges that his country has effectively become subservient to the United States. This not only would be a bitter pill to swallow but also would feed nationalist political and military elements within Russia that currently challenge Putin's agenda. The president has managed these groups so far, but a gesture of appeasement on this scale would inflame the passions of even the most pro-Western Russians. [47]

Another problem for America is the perception the Islamic world has of Russia and its treatment of Chechnya. America is anxious to distinguish itself from Russia in its current war with Al Qaeda and other terrorists. The War on Terrorism raised concerns in the Islamic community, and the US does not want to become any more of a target for terrorist assaults than it is currently. [48] Russia's war with Chechnya has damaged its credibility with Islamic countries, and China's conflict with the Uigur population and its separatists in Xinjiang, coupled with ongoing Israeli/Palestinian conflict gives plausibility to the argument that Islamic populations are really under attack. This furthers the perception that the Bush Administration chooses not to raise the Chechnya issue too strenuously because silence is part of the payoff for these nations cooperation. Clearly the US and NATO must do more than this to assure the Muslim community that they are indeed on their side and only against terrorists. [49] In fairness to Russia, they have *historically been harsh on all acts of domestic resistance, and military power has always been the means to solving this.* [50] This is clearly a mindset that views internal and external threats with the same disdain.

The US is continuing its foreign policy through NATO expansion in spite of the Russian mindset. Since the Russian military mindset requires all of it male citizens to serve in some capacity, scrutiny will be required when we look at how the military views its relationship with the civilian population and how the civilian population views the US and its allies. [51] Russia has clearly stated that NATO entry for the Baltic states, all former Soviet republics, will bring the alliance unacceptably close to its border. [52] Russia's military concerns are not without merit. The unique geography of Russia and lingering Cold War hostility, coupled with NATO expansion, has caused some communist alarmists in the top brass to view Western invasion as imminent. Anatol Lieven was quite perceptive when he wrote this is 1996,

> By saying I had not been to Moscow, I mean I had not fully appreciated the depths of Russian opposition to NATO expansion. In the case of the Baltic states, it would mean the effective dismantling of their north-western air-defense system, the isolation of their enclave of Kalininingrad; behind NATO's front line, complete abandonment of any political defense of the Baltic Russians, and their submitting to security dependence on the West.[53]

The inverse relationship between NATO expansion and Russian vulnerability is significant, and Russia has clearly stated its willingness to attack nuclear and non-nuclear states in order to defend itself and its allies. [54] In a similar way, America has recently responded to the War on Terrorism with a classified nuclear review that named Russia as one of the nations to be most concerned about. [55] Strangely enough, this news was not met by an outcry from Russia but somewhat of a yawning shrug. This is underscored by the fact that Russia has significant relations with all three countries named in Bush's Axis of Evil. All of these factors do not seem to be a hindrance to NATO's friendly disposition towards Russia. Gorbachev laid the foundation for expansion of NATO into Eastern Europe years ago because of the failure of military reform

Under Gorbachev, reform seized center stage. Moscow began to leave Eastern Europe alone and extend more autonomy to these regions at this time due to the fact they were not perceived as threats. The state of the military and economy came into full view during Gorbachev's reforms of Perestroika, New thinking and Glasnost. However, Gorbachev's plan backfired and gave rise to something else that is still cause for concern today in Russia, rapid reform without the proper mechanisms.[56] He virtually destroyed the very foundation and ideology of Soviet society by elevating human interests over the class struggle. Suddenly all of the nuclear weaponry assembled by the Soviets was no longer a cause for celebration, but caution and alarm. Nuclear weapons (according to Soviet propaganda directed at remaking their image) became a terrible thing and Russia's lead in the creation and placement of nuclear weapons, both tactical and missile based, strangely, suddenly, were no longer viewed as triumph of the worker class. Its conventional weapons remained formidable as well, but military power was effectively diminished in the eyes of Soviet citizens due to Gorbachev's reforms. [57] The decline continues, and the military itself began to be viewed differently, and the young men saw military duty as something to avoid at all costs, a sharp departure from previous generations. An all-volunteer force modeled after the US began to look appealing.

Conscription was the backbone of the military in the Soviet Union and the aim was to indoctrinate the male citizens into a way of viewing outsiders. Peter the Great's army of conscripts are still viewed as the model of the perfect army by many in Russia. The fact that virtually every able-bodied man served, in some capacity, solidified the unity between civilians and military personnel and the conscript based army was a symbol of the worker class in action, but problems persisted. The Soviets believed, erroneously, that continuing conscription would make conscripts dedicated to the Soviet cause. This would give rise to generational support of the military. Afghanistan proved this wrong, and many Central Asians who served in the war came back with tales of the brave Mujahadeen in Afghanistan. Military significance declined due to the relationship between its maintenance and a sound economic system. Military prestige came under fire with Glasnost (openness). Contemporary life in the Soviet military was horrible, and everyone in the top brass knew it, and now...the public would as well. The following problems: widespread hazing or dedovschina, drug abuse, suicide and murder were going to be exposed and for the first time ever; and the military would have to explain their behavior; the benefits of a closed system would not cover them. [58] In the meantime, the US was gearing up in order to display an AVF (All Volunteer Force) to the world.

The Gulf War was another blow that sent the Soviet military a strong message concerning US led NATO capability featuring AVFs versus Conscript based armies. The RMA (Revolution in Military Affairs) of Desert Storm brought about a change in the way wars are fought. The USSR was taken aback by the accuracy of the awesome firepower that the US and its NATO allies unleashed in this war. The swift decisive blows that Saddam Hussein suffered were enough to bring the World's fourth largest army to its knees within the snap of the fingers. Clearly amateurs could not do this. So the next step for Russia would be to try to emulate the US and NATO through the use of pseudo volunteers, termed as a contract soldiers. Years of attempted reform and the failure of the contract soldier yielded no promising results for the future. The contract soldiers were a pitiful Russian version of a professional force. NATO's superior technology and forces during the Iraq conflict caused alarm and paranoia throughout Russia. The days of a reliable conscript soldier were over, and the West superior execution and highly trained soldier became the new prototype for the future. [59]

The Western model of an AVF flew in the face of a conscription based model and mindset. The altar of communism previously served to justify the loss of nearly 70 million lives when the following were combined: WWI, The Bolshevik Revolution, WWII, and Stalin's ruthless purges. Previously this idea justified the way and course of the nation. The crushing defeat of Gorbachev's reforms and the abandonment of communism were too much for many in the top brass to stomach. In short, Gorbachev erased the idea of a terrible enemy with insatiable greed waiting to takeover the world. Eastern Europe was not listening either. Many of these conscripts loss their lives for mother Russia and communism and were viewed as heroes and symbols of resistance. The idea that the West is casualty averse and Russia is not, fueled the idea that limited nuclear war was winnable, but now all of those notions were erased.

Every Soviet leader before him had rejected peaceful coexistence with the West, at least publicly. NATO was not only a symbol of capitalist aggression; it was viewed as THE INSTRUMENT of such aggression and the harbinger of death to Communism. Preparing for the imminent threat of a military conflict with NATO rallied the troops and provided a guiding ideology for Russian/Soviet society. Gorbachev was slowly overturning this, and further he pushed for something more...cooperation with the West, economically, culturally and militarily as far as arms reductions. [60]

Resistance to his plans was well documented, and many of the hardliners/old-timers longed for simpler times, and some actually believed in the communist dream of a social utopia. The military was the guiding force of such change, and war was an extension of the worker class justice. They needed enemies to legitimize their place, and NATO and the US were those enemies. Gorbachev's opponents in military leadership and the DUMA had to find a way to keep the status quo, but they failed. The military professionals had other ideas about reform and were doing everything in their power to render his plan obsolete. They were wait-ing for something to happen; either the recovery of the economy or the appear-ance of a strategic enemy would do the trick. When one or the other occurred, it would build societal support for the military, and enable them to reclaim some of the prestige they lost during Gorbachev's perestroika. [61] They were waiting then, and some are waiting now.

The Gulf war brought into question many aspects of Soviet military doctrine and changed the way Russia views it security. As it scrambled to create a new force that could withstand the disintegration of the Soviet Union and ward off NATO influence, it cited some changes that needed to take place, particularly, 6 military-technical dimensions were embraced:

1. the character of the threat

2. the type of struggle that may evolve

3. the requirements for defense

4. the armed forces required

5. the means to conduct armed forces and struggles

6. preparation of the forces to accomplish these purposes. [62]

The meaning behind these six points is not vague or ambiguous, but straight forward and clear, but no matter how clear a doctrine is, it doesn't always serve the purpose it is intended to serve. The Russians saw American air power and technology at work during the gulf war and concluded that all future wars would be fought in this way.

Ideas about warfare have changed in Russia. More recently they have been driven home by Russian failure in Chechnya. The conflict in Chechnya reveals some glaring weaknesses of the Russian army and the conscript system. When viewing the Western model, Russia clearly saw the strengths that the West pos-sessed and wanted to have a similar military. Their contract soldiers numbered at roughly 270,000 in 96—including a number of women, 50% of them officer's wives. The cost was roughly 5 times as much as that of a conscript, given the fact payment is already 5 to 6 months behind and 120,000 contract soldiers are homeless, one could see why this wouldn't be a popular job. The economics aren't the only problems that would hinder the recruitment of more contract sol-diers. [63]

Putin inherited a military where nearly 80% of the conscripts available for the draft will try to find a way out, only 50% have completed secondary school and 15% are not medically fit while 5% carry criminal records. This is the current progress toward the idea of an AVF. It is an idea that surfaces in the Russian dialogue concerning what needs to be done, but quickly disappears due to the resistance of the military leadership. The years of military reform have passed Russia by without producing any substantial alternative to conscription. The military leadership resisted the idea from the beginning, and the reasons seem to be good ones, the economy, public duty, the necessity for manpower, and geographical vulnerability. [64] To say Russia doesn't have the money for conventional forces that could thwart NATO expansion is rather obvious, but it remains an oversimplification of a very complex problem. The core problem is how Russia views the US and the rather easy justification for the use of nuclear weapons. The last century has taught them to expect the worse in war and to view their enemies as willing to use these nukes first. This has developed a beat them to the punch mentality. [65]

Recent declassified reports revealed nearly a dozen situations in the 80s and early 90s in which Russia put their nuclear forces on high alert, because they viewed a strike from the US as imminent. Further, even domestic disturbances and unrest became reasons for Russia to pay more attention to the potential exploitation of these crises from the West. Tending to its own problems are secondary issues for its leadership. [66] Since the decline of its forces and low military morale keep Russia from being a credible threat to NATO with conventional weapons, Russia continues to expect Western forces to strike at it while it remains in this vulnerable state, and further, Russia is aware that many of its former neighbors in Eastern Europe would be all too happy to assist the US and NATO in a war against its former oppressors.

Conclusion

The top brass and political leadership in Russia are fearful and paranoid. Historically Russia has always been slow to move forward and change, until some national calamity brings them together, or they achieve some new vision for their country. Mobilization of the Russian people usually requires the very real or imagined presence of some enemy that will attack them mercilessly, giving rise to mass fear and paranoia and military mobilization. The Mongolians, Swiss, Polish, Turks and Germans all left their imprint on Russia, and the vestiges of these conflicts and wars form the basis of the distrust of others endemic within the Russian worldview. Since they will not trust US intentions, America must respond in kind.

The Reality of the Russian/Western experience is this...the West progresses, and the East lags behind. Russian intention of attacking the US with nuclear weapons if it perceives itself in danger remains intact. It still remains inferior in many areas. Russia has lived with the reality that the US is superior and can live with it, while continuing to pursue parity. But it would be a mistake to try and reverse the course and not continue to remind Russia of its secondary place in the world, the fact that its former satellites yearn for democracy and refuse to be subjected to it and that the entire world is looking west. It is clear that Russia must cooperate with the West while it is in a place of weakness. Russia respects strength. That said, the policy should be one not of containment alone, but invitation to be Western as well. Russia could possibly continue to experiment with democracy and improve its human rights record and give greater civil liberty to its citizens.

For now, the historical pattern should suffice, and it seems to reveal a resiliency pattern of defeat and resurgence that consistently revives Russia and places them on center stage in World events. The phrase, "a resurgent Russia" can cause military and civilian analysts to shudder. No one wants to relive the Cold War, or move into a Cold Peace, but that is a poor reason to pretend all is well between Russia and America. The *Bear* will be back, and he will slap the vinegar off the diplomatic table, demanding honey instead.

NOTES

1.William Green, Interview, Professor of Eurasian Studies, Cal State University, San Bernardino (Lt. Commander, Naval Forces, May, 21, 2002)

2.Odom, William. The Collapse Of The Soviet Military (New Haven: Con.: Yale University Press,1998) pp. 131–33

3 Ibid

4. Tatiana Parkhalina, "Of myths and illusions: Russian perceptions of NATO enlargement," *NATO Review* Vol. 45 No. 3 (May-June 1997), pp. 11–15.

5. International Development and Research Center, "Human Security and Mutual Vulnerability," IDRC, CA. September 1999

6. Purdum, Todd S., NATO Strikes Deal To Accept Russia In A Partnership New York Times, May 15, 2002 Pg.

7. Foreign & Security Policy of Ukraine, "Russian Security Discourse and NATO Enlargement: A View From Russia: Occasional Paper 3, 1998 </1998-01ope03ruwe-natoenlargement.phtml>

8. Ibid

9. Herspring, Dale R. Russian Civil-Military Relations, (Indiana University Press, 1996) p. 134

10. Robert Marquand "US quickens China-Russia thaw" Chinese news agency warned yesterday that US missile shield plans could start an arms race" <http://fas.org/nuke/control/abmt/chron.htm> Christian Science Monitor May 3, 2001 It should be noted as well that unipolar means that one country dominates the international system, economically and militarily. During the days of the Cold war the world was viewed as bipolar with the US/USSR relationship sharing influence in all spheres. Multi polar is where several major powers have great influence in world events.

11.Foreign & Security Policy of Ukraine, "Russian Security Discourse..."

12.Federation of American Scientists, "Chronology Anti-Ballistic Missile Defense Treaty"

13. Ibid

14. Purdum, Todd S., NATO Strikes Deal To Accept Russia In A Partnership New York Times, May 15, 2002

15. The International Institute For Strategic Studies. The Military Balance 1997–98 (Oxford University Press, 1998)

16. Purdum, Todd S., NATO Strikes Deal To Accept Russia...

17. Fischer, Beth A. The Reagen Reversal: Foreign Policy And The End Of The Cold War (University of Missouri Press, Columbia Missouri, 1997 p.76–77

18. Ibid

19. STRATFOR, "Crisis Looms Between U.S., Russia, 20 March 2002"

20. Ibid

21. Hyland, William, "NATO: The Next Generation" (Westview Press, 1984)

22. Dmitri Trenin, "Avoiding a new confrontation with NATO" *by* <u>NATO Review</u>—May 1996

23. Russian Military Doctrine 1999

24. Anatol Lieven, "Baltic Iceberg Dead Ahead: NATO Beware," *The World Today*, July

25. Odom, William. The Collapse Of The Soviet Military pp. 100, 120

26. Ibid

27. Scheurweghs, Chris, Study On NATO Enlargement September 1995 NATO INTEGRATED DATA SERVICE (NIDS

28. Brewer, Anthony Marxist Theories Of Imperialism: A Critical Survey: Second Edition. (Routledge, London and New york, 1990) Introductionp. 1–11

29. Tatiana Parkhalina,"Of myths and illusions: Russian perceptions of NATO enlargement"—<u>NATO Review</u>—*May-June 1997*

30. Russian Military Draft Doctrine 1999

31. Richard Kugler, *Enlarging NATO: The Russian Factor* (Santa Monica, CA: Rand, 1996).

32. Ibid

33. Perlmutter, Amos and Ted Galen Carpenter, "NATO's Expensive Trip East: The Folly Of Enlargement," *Foreign Affairs* Vol. 77 (January-February 1998), pp. 2–6. (note this article is not in favor of Nato Expansion but it points to our concerns about them)

34. Bodie, William C., "Moscows Near Abroad Security policy in Post-Soviet Europe", Europe National Defense University, (Mc Nair Paper Sixteen June 1993

35. Brandenburg, Ulrich "NATO and Russia: A natural partnership" NATO Review, July-August 1997

36. Marshal Igor Sergeye, We are not Adversaries, We are Partners—<u>NATO Review</u>—Spring *1998*

37. Lieven, Antanol, "Nato and the Baltics: Two opposing views" (City Paper—The Baltic States, Summer,1996)

38. Ibid.

39. Tyler, Patrick, E, "Baltic States See NATO as Shield From Russia" New York Times International, June 15th 2001 <u>http://www.nytimes.com</u>

40. STRATFOR, "Crisis Looms Between U.S., Russia, 20 March 2002"

41. Bodie, William C. "Moscows Near Abroad Security policy in Post-Soviet Europe", Europe National Defense University (Mc Nair Paper Sixteen June 1993
42. Fuller, William C Jr. Strategy and Power in Russia, 1660–1940 (New York: The Free Press,1992
43. Ibid.
44. Green, William, C, Interview, Cal State University San Bernadino, May, 21, 2002
45. STRATFOR, "Crisis Looms Between U.S., Russia, 20 March 2002"
46. Ibid
47. Anatol Lieven, "Baltic Iceberg Dead Ahead: NATO Beware," *The World Today*, July
48.Breffni, O'Rourke, "Baltics: NATO Membership Is Divisive Issue Free Europe.
49. Bunker, Robert, Hazim, Hakim "Foreign Opfor Reader Occasional Paper #3: Radical Islamic Doctrine", (NLECTC-West, April, 2002)
50. Kipp, Jacob W. "Russian Military Reform: Status and Prospects(Views Of A Western Military Historian)
51. Breffni, O'Rourke, "Baltics: NATO Membership Is Divisive Issue Free Europe)
52. Anatol Lieven, "Baltic Iceberg Dead Ahead: NATO Beware," "*The World Today*, July
53. Ibid.
54. Russian Military Doctrine, 1999
55. STRATFOR, "Crisis Looms Between U.S., Russia, 20 March 2002"
56. Odom, William. The Collapse Of The Soviet Military (New Haven: Con.: Yale University Press,1998) pp. 130–53
57. Ibid
58. Herspring, Dale R. Russian Civil-Military Relations, (Indiana University Press, 1996) pp. 190–212
59. Felker, Edward J. "Oz Revisited: Russian Military Doctrinal Reform in the light of Desert Storm"School Of Advanced Airpower Studies, Air University Maxwell Air Force Base, Alabama. Jun 94)
60. Hazim, Hakim, "The Russian Military Mindset": Graduate Paper, Summer 2000,
61. Brewer, Anthony Marxist Theories Of Imperialism: A Critical Survey: (Second Edition. Routledge, London and New york, 1990) 70–73

62. Felker, Edward J. "Oz Revisted: Russian Military Doctrinal Reform in the light of Desert Storm"School Of Advanced Airpower Studies, Air University Maxwell Air Force Base, Alabama. Jun 94)

63. Dick, C J. "Russian Military Reform: Status and Prospects" (Conflict Studies Research Centre,1998)

64. Ibid

65. Russian Military Doctrine 1999

66. Pry, Peter, *War Scare*,(Library of Congress Cataloging-in-Publication Data,1999) p.13

Russia Rising: Patterns of Military Reform as an Impetus for Nationalism

Hakim Hazim

© *February 2003*

In the past, *"The very things that made Russia backward and underdeveloped by comparison with Western Europe-autocracy, serfdom, poverty-could paradoxically be translated into armed might."* [1]

Authors comments: Will Russia's relative backwardness, resistant transition to democracy, continued conscription and need for a visible enemy cause it to emerge again and balance America's unipolarity, and if so is America and the West ready for the challenges? When contrasted with the wealth and relatively easy life of the West, Russia's hardened citizenry may be ready to endure major conflict once again. East and West are once again juxtaposed with different aims and different means to gaining their goals.

Two major Russian military draft doctrines of 1993 and 2000, revealed a paradigm shift in the thinking of the military leadership in Russia. It reflected a look within and without, but not far away. Russia still viewed the US and NATO as its primary threat, but has acknowledged in 1993, and in subsequent draft doctrines, that its nearby neighbors could pose serious security problems. NATO has grafted in some of those nearby neighbors. This threat, perceived or real, will fuel the resurgence of Russia. Russia needs an enemy because the history of its people is one of suffering, warfare and resurgence. By looking to the past, the author hopes to show overconfidence on the part of Russia's enemies has proven to be catastrophic. This is a mistake America can ill afford to repeat. Russia has stated that it is primarily interested in internal security, and there is a reason for this. The need for cohesion within during this transnational period is foundational if Russia is to revive into a superpower once more. Here is a list of the concerns and obstacles they are seeking to overcome that were highlighted in 2000 and remain.

The following statements taken from the 2000 draft doctrine highlight Russian concerns

Basic internal threats:

1. Securing Russia from: *"the violent overthrow of the constitutional system; activities of extremist national-ethnic, religious separatist and terrorist movements, organizations and structures aimed at disrupting state unity, and territorial integrity and at destabilizing the internal situation in the Russian Federation"*
2. The need destroy internal threats who are engaged in the: *"planning, preparation and accomplishment of actions to disrupt and disorganize the functioning of bodies of state authority and management, and of attacks on state, national economic, military, life support and information infrastructure installations"*

3. Stopping the unlawful groups from gaining access to: *"equipment, training and functioning of unlawful armed units; proliferation (circulation) on Russian Federation territory of weapons, ammunition, explosives and other means which can be used for carrying out sabotage, terrorist acts, and other unlawful actions."*
4. Curtailing: *"crime, terrorism, smuggling and other unlawful activity on a scale threatening Russian Federation military security. Ensuring military security.*[2]*"*

The main provisions of the 2000 Military draft doctrine focus on the transitional period Russia is currently facing. This transitional period of Russia is a time in which Russia claims they are seeking the transformation to a democratic society that possesses a multi-structured economy. [3] In 2000, Russia's military doctrine focused on internal and external threats while calling specific attention to illegally armed groups within the Russian Federation. Russia remains consistent in its claims that it seeks to militarily challenge "and eliminate unlawful armed units, bandit, terrorist groups, organizations, and their bases, training centres, depots and lines of communication."[2000 Military Draft Doctrine] This doctrine is fully focused on decreasing these threats. It tones down the rhetoric of regional wars spreading to other nations, declaring the threat of World War as unlikely. The 2000 Russian Military Doctrine was crafted with two purposes in mind: ending the Chechen conflict and creating a multi-polar world; to date, neither have occurred, but Russia continues to pursue this course.

The war in Chechnya is Russia's *stated* priority; in reality it must deal with this threat before it can be a great world power. It calls for cooperation between its law enforcement communities and military when dealing with the likelihood of continued armed resistance within Russian borders and drafts an appropriate doctrine with provisions that seek this end. The differences in Russia's 93 and 2000 military doctrines were crafted for the purpose of ending the Chechen conflict, the main "unlawful armed unit" within its territory, and as already stated, the 2000 doctrine also seeks the creation of a multi-polar world, to this end, Russia is pursuing allies. Russia is currently set on healing an old rift with China and exporting nuclear technology and arms to Iran, India and possibly North Korea.

The 2000 doctrine supports a multipolar world and views unipolarity as a threat to world security; yet, it does not view NATO expansion as a Western means to imminent invasion? One can hardly take these statements at face value. This is a way of simply appeasing the US in light of Russia's momentary weakness. This is simply a doctrine that backs off from tired rhetoric of previous threats that placed a great deal of emphasis on the use of nuclear weapons in an effort to safeguard its territory. Russia continues to advocate the use of nuclear deterrence, but it reverses its 93 position by stating a no-first-strike policy, previously adhered to by the USSR. The doctrine also states a desire for the gradual eradication of nuclear weapons on a global scale; this is a refurbished Gorbachev idea. Part of Russia's concern for tempering its position on nuclear weapons and advocating reductions is due to the post-Cold War nature of the world, its inability to disarm without Western aid, and its inability to sufficiently oversee all of its nuclear stockpile, particularly its tactical or battlefield nukes. Further, Russia is more than a little concerned about the emerging threat of terrorism and foreign groups supplying aid to armed groups within its borders, and specifically, Al Qaeda's stated desire to acquire these weapons, giving rise to fears of a growing nexus between terrorist groups and the breakaway republic of Chechnya.

In the 93 draft doctrine the language specifically stated that Russia would use nuclear weapons to defend itself against non-nuclear nations and extend its nuclear deterrence to its allies. The draft doctrine of 93 also stated that the greatest threat to its security was likely to arise from internal threats; it also focused a great deal of attention on NATO expansion. This doctrine was based on the relative weakness of the Russian Federation's conventional weapons and the inevitability of NATO expansion. Russia's threats failed to deter. [4] In 93 Russia's primary focus was threatening its neighbors and NATO with nuclear weapons if it perceived it sovereign territory was being encroached upon. Later, most of these nuclear threats proved to be irrelevant as the nation was inexplicably embroiled in a conflict with Chechnya that both humiliated and deprived the military of any status it had left in the minds of its citizens and former enemies in the West. The current reform has ideas from Russia's past that certainly require diligent study. The relevance of the Milutin reforms has many lessons for the West. Milutin reforms will give us an idea of where Russia is headed militarily.

Milutin reforms did not suddenly appear from the ether; they were a continuation, an extension of Russian domestic and foreign policy that has always been concerned about its military strength and its relative backwardness when compared with the West. The West is Russia's canon concerning modernization, and all of its reformers had this in mind when they sought to move their nation forward. William Hyland asserts that the history of Russian expansionism, modernization, reform and foreign policy dates back to Peter the Great's desire for parity with the West. [5] Hyland writes about an ensuing "Russian national psychology" that caused the people to rally behind any czar figure when the masses believe that Mother Russia was in danger. This is followed up by the historical record of the 19th century suffering that Russia has endured under WW1, The Bolshevik

Revolution, WWII and Stalin's purges. These examples lead Hyland to conclude, "In defending Mother Russia, they have an unparalleled capacity for suffering." [6] The resiliency cycle of the Russian people will cause military reform to go forward with a greater degree of success than previous changes, because "every military mirrors the strengths and weaknesses of its society…" and Russia appears to be preparing for resurgence in spite of it relative backwardness. [7]

During the mid 1800s Russia found itself lagging behind the West once again, and statesmen sought a way to move forward in spite of the internal problems. In 1861 Grand Duke Konstantin began to implement sweeping reforms, including the liberation of serfs. His newly appointed Minister of War, Dimitry Milyutin, was of a similar mindset and saw a need to graft the newly liberated populations into the new military he would build. Milyutin reforms were born out of the need for Russia to move its population forward. Russia knew it needed to modernize, and Milyutin wanted to use technology in order to prepare the soldiers for better tactical and strategic war and ideology as a means to unify the population. Russia had its share of domestic problems as a result of serfdom and the consequences that accompanied it. One consequence for instance was the tremendous gaps between the haves and have-nots, giving rise to rebellions and riots. [8] Milyutin reforms had two primary ideas:

1. He wanted to graft the serfs into the military in hopes of creating brotherhood between the classes and mitigating the influence of class structure, which would hopefully lead to internal order and stability because of military discipline they would learn and its presence throughout the country.

2. He sought to produce a stronger army that could defend and invade, because serfdom produced a soldier that could outlast the most well trained Western soldier due to the hardships and deprivations associated with a serf's lot in life.

Milyutin sought to bring the military up to date and the peasant's spirits soaring through renewed patriotism and nationalism

As minister of war, he was more liberal and idealistic than his predecessors—perhaps due to his relatively low birth-when he looked at common people. He believed that other nations were drawing more from their people in industrial and military affairs than Russia, and he sought to emulate the West in this matter. He sought to change the country's military through reforms. These reforms would include changes in the following: recruiting, manner of discipline and training, physical environment in which combat would be fought, opening mili-

tary schools to non-nobles, implementing Western laws, establishing better transport and communications systems, and last of all abolishing corporal punishment
in times of peace. Milyutin understood the fact that the military could only
reflect the very best and worse of the society that gave birth to it. As an extension
of that society, he understood that effective war waging required a process that
would mobilize the entire society for warfare. To this end he sought to indoctrinate the people of Russia into a *Rechtsstaat*, "a state founded on the impartial and
consistent administration of the laws." [9]

Milyutin, like Peter the Great and others before him, believed that the whole
of society had to be shaped and formed in order to provide the right glue to its
unity, due to Russia's geographical vulnerability and their history of warfare
against Austria, Poland, Germany and other nations or coalitions. Milyutin formulated a long-term approach to defending Russia against the perceived aggressive enemies on its borders during "The Strategic Conference of 1873". Milutin
and other strategists and policy-makers believed that they were likely to be
invaded by a coalition of enemies, and this mindset remains with Russia to this
day. [10] To offset this he sought a plan that included "…sophisticated armaments,
fortifications and a strategic railway network." This plan was never implemented,
and an ad hoc interim strategy that relied on backwardness was crafted. [11]

Russia has continually unified its people and military by pointing to imminent
threats of invasion from enemies, but a dubious fact emerges from the pages of
history. The fact of the matter is this, historians can only point to one or two
wars that Russia has engaged in defensively. Most of what Russia had termed
defensive battles included the continued use of preemption. Preemption was the
fruit of a historical mind-set that produced Russia's harsh interactions with its
neighbors and remains with Russia today. In Soviet times the Russian military
mindset was a worldview that called for a readiness and willingness to defend
Russian sovereignty no matter the cost, and this mind-set was effectively trans-
ferred to all of its citizens, and communism was the means to achieving this
indoctrination. [12] This mindset stated that every citizen must participate in the
war machine to varying degrees. The draft, designed by Milyutin, continued to
this day, appears to be another way of transferring this mind-set.

In 1874 Milyutin believed that the newly freed serfs owed the country something. He instituted the universal draft. His hope was that this new manpower
would be sufficient enough to move the war machine and add a dimension of
patriotism to the ranks. His expectations had mixed results. Russian soldiers did
prove to have an amazing capacity for suffering, but the loyalty he expected did
not materialize. Previously, the loyalty of the peasant was given to his family, now

he was told to transfer this, automatically and instantaneously, to his fellow countryman and the Tsar. There was no such transition and the end result of this was manifested in full force in 1917. Milyutin decided to forfeit the advantages of backwardness so aptly developed by Peter the Great and his generals, and replaced it with nothing of substance.

For the best view of backwardness being implemented in a sound strategic way, one must look even further into the pages of history to Peter the Great's day and time. His reign was filled with internal and external conflict, but he changed Russia by dragging it from the Dark ages and into a fairly modern era. Peter fully utilized the backwardness of his nation to win the Great Northern War. Although the King of Sweden's (Charles VII) army was powerful and well trained, it was also loaded with mercenaries and could only afford a few casualties. Peter the Great was able to fight a long protracted war that cost a high number of causalities, and saw large numbers of deserters as well, but these were people he could replace rather easily because of the large numbers of serfs he could readily draw from. Peter's military was poorly trained and ill equipped to effectively wage warfare the European way, but it was effective nonetheless. Standing armies consisted of well trained, fed, paid, and in some cases literate citizen-soldiers and mercenaries. Peter's army was comprised of simple, drafted, peasants who possessed a thorough knowledge of the land, willingness to make use of simple weapons and tools, willingness to die, and unrivalled capacity for suffering. Peter could fight a relatively cheap war and throw countless bodies at an enemy who entered Russian territory. In fact, the territory that the serfs were use to living, rather, surviving on, had hardened them to their environment; conversely, the land itself became an enemy for the Swiss, as many perished in this harsh environment. Some of these factors of backwardness remain today, but Russia has not been able to take advantage of them and continues to seek a Western type reform first mentioned by Mikhail Gorbachev.

In modern day terms, military reform first seized center stage under Gorbachev. Gorbachev believed that he had to move the USSR forward and out of the backwardness of its day, but he failed to realize the unintended consequences of such a gamble...the end of the USSR. The sad reality is this, the large percentage of money dedicated to the MIC effectively churned out nuclear and conventional weapons while domestic programs were neglected. Communism as a system was proven suspect as the threat of imminent invasion from the West and images of capitalistic hordes storming into Russia after a nuclear exchange eventually lost its hold on the people. To date, no significant progress in military reform has been made. Gorbachev implemented a three-layered approach for his plan and approach to take root.

Gorbachev's reforms of Perestroika, New thinking and Glasnost were aimed at reforming society, but in order to do that he would have to reform the military because the two were inexplicably linked. However, Gorbachev's plan backfired and gave rise to something else that is still cause for concern today, rapid reform without the proper mechanisms. [13] He virtually destroyed the very foundation and ideology of Soviet society by elevating human interests over the class struggle. Suddenly all of the nuclear weaponry assembled by the Soviets was no longer a cause for celebration, but caution and alarm. Nuclear weapons (according to Soviet propaganda directed at remaking their image) became a terrible thing, and Russia's lead in the creation and placement of nuclear weapons, both tactical and missile based, strangely, suddenly, were no longer viewed as a triumph of the worker class. Its conventional weapons remained formidable as well, but military prestige was effectively diminished in the eyes of Soviet citizens due to Gorbachev's reforms. Soon the viscous that held Russian nationality together was shattered and nothing was left to replace it. Milyutin had something to offer the newly liberated population of serfs, inclusion in the society via conscription.

Milyutin's universal conscription had a two-fold purpose: building up the reserves for peacetime and wartime forces, and secondly for purposes of greater inclusion. He also believed that all citizens had to buy into *Rechtsstaat*, (as stated earlier a nation founded on the impartiality and consistent administration of laws). In order to achieve this, he wanted to strip some of the privilege from certain nobles and bolster a national patriotism that was indifferent to class. This stripping took place to a greater degree and was a precursor of something Russia instituted much later in Communism.[14] In reality the draft remains in place because it is a mechanism for reinforcing nationalism. The universal draft is still in place and with some of the same problems Russia has historically faced, but an explosion of others as well. The numbers of troops avoiding service continues to skyrocket and the numbers of deserters continues as well. It would appear that Russia's backwardness continues in military terms to this day with the crisis of national identity remaining as well. [15] The question that remains is this, will those reforms end as Milutin's did or will the new reforms prove effective?

Milutin's reforms failed to realize its potential during his time and largely due to the industrial expertise of its Western neighbors and the squandered economic opportunities of Alexander II. Western countries featured advanced citizenry, economies, transportation and communication capabilities and some democratic processes that released the true potential of the citizenry of advanced nations. [16]

Russia is struggling with this today and attempting to form a more forward moving society that unleashes the potential of its citizens, while crafting out an ideology that the people can rally around. Military reform has often been the impetus for sweeping changes in Russian society before, but there must be a threat, real and present, in order for the people to rally around such reforms.

Touching and reforming the draft system that Milutin implemented could be akin to touching something sacred in the minds of Russia's military leadership; therefore, the system of conscription will remain, and reform will be limited. Russians will continue to look for ways to improve their military, and they may even relax draft requirements, but they will never approach an all-volunteer force. In short, the Russian leadership is unwilling to give up the idea of conscription, and the contract soldier is akin to a slothful, halfhearted mercenary. Russia's experiment with the contract/professional soldier has borne the following fruit: mental dullness (the inability to carry out complex orders or use weapons safely), and alcoholism. There is also criminal behavior from ex-convicts who are looking for the opportunity to sell off weapons, and in some cases, soldiers who are psychopaths and want the opportunity to kill. [17] Russia's search for new military and societal ideas continues, and those ideas wrested from Milyutin reforms and blended into Marxism are looking for a home once again.

Conclusion: It can be argued that Milyutin ideas found a home in Communism and Russia seeks to put the ideas to work today

Rechtsstaat is defined as a system of laws that are just and therefore obligatory for all people within a state or group. As an idea it remains relevant in Russia today. Conscription is a part of that idea, because it places an obligation on its entire population to not only follow the laws of the land without partiality; it also commands them to defend the way of life the laws uphold. In fact it remains the backbone of the military fighting force, because the leaders believe this will cause people to buy into and support the society they are attempting to rebuild and defend after the collapse of communism. All societies understand the power of ideas.

Seven levels of ideas (The authors philosophical construct, see introduction):

1. Ideas are birthed and accepted as plausible or rejected.

2. If accepted they are placed into philosophical constructs.

3. Powerful individuals or groups migrate towards these ideas and create momentum or movements.

4. Conflicting ideas between groups lead to conflict or compromise. In some cases the ideas are incorporated into an already existing philosophy and at other times, during an impasse, the conflict may become physical in nature, resulting in war.

5. The emerging winner bases the group or nation on the idea or philosophy.

6. Laws will be passed reflecting these ideas.

7. The state or group enforces these laws.

The idea of class struggle worked for a people with a history of serfdom and struggle. Communism provided these as an extension of Milyutin's desire to organize the society and remove the status of privilege. Some ideas perished at the end of the Cold War, and the glue that held society together needed to be replaced by something. New groups are emerging in an effort to replace the eroding values of communism. The parallels between *Rechtsstaat* and communism remain. *Rechtsstaat* was part of an ongoing attempt to unify all of the Russian people around a single idea, and that struggle remains today. For now, authoritarian, oppressive leaders will have to do, as Russia continues to pursue a *Rechsstaat* society.

Russians have a history of responding to cruel oppressive leaders, which seems to be the only way of getting the people to respond. Perhaps it is the nature of Russians to seek an external force to control their population. Dr. William Green elaborated on Russian folklore with the story of a group of Slavs in the Early Middle Ages who told a foreign invader, "We have gold, land and goods but no ruler. Come and rule over us. [18] This process of external control, versus autonomy within the heart of the citizens, sheds light on a perplexing problem. In order to fully understand this process the Russian triangle should be visited.

Vladimir Pastukhov paper, "The End of Postcommunism: Perspectives on Russian Reformers" addresses this issue in detail. The Russian triangle is an explanation of the workings of Russia and the relationship between the state authority, the reform movement and society. Pastukhov states that in the past Russian society was passive and oriented toward the state. In this role the state and society represented a static subsystem that curbed any dangerous, fluctuating political events. The reform movement represents a different part of the triangle and vies for the loyalty of the society at large, but all understand that in order to change the society, the military mind-set must be changed. [19] Milyutin reform sought to change the society as a whole by using military reform. Gorbachev followed the same path, and in the future Russia will continue the same pattern.

In the past, Russia's military leaders have acted as galvanizing forces in Russian history, and many look for "a man on horseback" to lead them out of times of trouble, desperation and tribulation. [20] This man on horseback can demand extraordinary sacrifices of the people; they will be willing to suffer if they believe their nation is in danger, and the outcome is worth it. Political leaders will exploit this in an effort to turn Russia around again. What Russia may need is a crisis. Let us hope one is not manufactured soon.

Notes

1. Fuller, William C. Jr., Strategy and Power in Russia, 1660–1940 (New York: The Free Press, 1992) pp. 82–83

2. Hyland, William "NATO: The Next Generation" (Westview Press, 1984).

3. Ibid

4. Fuller, William C. Jr., *Strategy and Power in Russia,* 1660–1940 (New York: The Free Press,1992) pp. 281–82

5. Ibid.

6. Ibid.

7. Nik, Zherve, *Graf, D. A. Miliutin: Biograficheskii ocherk* (St. Ptersberg, 1906) pp. 11–10

8. Fuller, p.306

9. Kipp, Jacob W. "Russian Military Reform: Status and Prospects: Views Of A Western Military Historian"

10. Odom, William. The Collapse Of The Soviet Military (New Haven: Con.: Yale University Press,1998) pp. 131–33

11. Fuller, 305

12. Felgenhauer, Pavel "Russian Military Reform: Ten years of Failure", Sevodnya, Moscow

13. Vladimir Pastukhov "The End Of Postcommunism: Perspectives on Russian Reformers"

14. Mackinnon, Mark "Learning to dodge the draft in Russia" Copyright © 2002 Bell Globemedia Interactive Inc.

15. Pavel Felgenhauer, "Most Righteous War of All" The Moscow Times Thursday, Feb. 13, 2003. Page 9

16. Dick, C J. "Russian Military Reform: Status and Prospects",(Conflict Studies Research Centre,1998)

17. MYERS, STEVEN LEE, "Russian Group Is Offering Values to Fill a Void", The New York Times, February 16, 2003

18. Green, William, Regional Security of Eurasia, Seminar CSUSB Spring 2000

19.Vladimir Pastukhov "The End Of Postcommunism: Perspectives on Russian Reformers

20. Ibid

Shiism Unleashed: Oppression, Occupation and Deliverance in Iraq

Hakim Hazim

© *July 2005*

These terrorists target the innocent, and they kill by the thousands. And they would, if they gain the weapons they seek, kill by the millions and not be finished. The greatest threat of our age is nuclear, chemical, or biological weapons in the hands of terrorists, and the dictators who aid them. The evil is in plain sight. The danger only increases with denial. <u>Great responsibilities fall once again to the great democracies.</u> We will face these threats with open eyes, and we will defeat them

President George Bush, Royal Banqueting House-Whitehall Palace, London England, November 19, 2003

That is a chilling quote; one stated to arouse fear, but after all was said and done Iraq has not produced any palpable weapons of mass destruction. A skeptical world continues to muse over statements like these from the Bush administration. The press, critics and political analysts continue to press the administration for answers. The Islamic world is not just asking; it's demanding answers and timetables, while our allies reexamine their positions. This is the current state of affairs and the reality that America faces. In my view, there was always more at stake in Iraq than these statements before and after the invasion. Two primary goals were established before the invasion took place: ousting Iraq's dictator and securing another place of influence in the Middle East. The question was never if, only when and how to move. Saddam is in prison so that mission is accomplished, but the battle for political power and influence rages on. Swirling in the center of this struggle are ideological winds. There are three tempests with supranational aims, and Iraq has become the primary symbol of this struggle. The three impetuses at work are:

1. American forces attempting to establish **democracy** throughout the region according to Bush's view that democracy is a birthright

2. Al Qaeda, its message and the hub of supranational and regional terrorist actively converting others to their version of **global jihad**

3. An emerging Shiite community with ties to Iran's Shiites, giving rise to **Shiism** as a political force in the Middle East and beyond

The forces are colliding on a daily basis, and a clear winner has not emerged. Democratic principles such as free elections are goals that can realistically be established, but the Wolfolwitzian worldview of the Bush administration binds them to the idea they can democratize Iraq. They fail to recognize that the likely outcome of such elections will give rise to a political Shia movement with regional and supranational implications. Saddam was an oppressive, secular tyrant who did not supply his people with any ideology. Tyranny and totalitarianism are incompatible with democracy, and this has caused this administration to express a desire to end tyranny by advancing democracy in the world by undoubtedly starting with Iraq. Such lofty statements are nothing more than yearning idealism and will prove extremely difficult to establish, due to the fact totalitarianism is the normal rule for many governments outside of the West.[1]

Iraq: Transitioning from Totalitarianism to Free Elections

Totalitarian states control the individual and espouse the belief that all should be totally subject to the state. Totalitarian regimes and ideologies deliberately attempt to control the thinking of citizens through indoctrination and the use of severe punitive measures against those who openly dissent. These tactics become part of the culture and are easily carried over by the new leadership, even elected leadership. Iraq was a secular, totalitarian regime that was based on Saddam's personality and centralized control of the Baath party. Religious fervor was not tolerated, and the Shiites were oppressed. Totalitarian ideologies and regimes are oppressive and still exist in places other than Islamic countries. The personalities and statesmen in charge of such nations have instituted fear as the primary means of controlling and motivating their populations, and the legacies left behind are troublesome and difficult to overcome when the dictator is removed, or the ideology fails. This was the case in Russia, Eastern Europe and Central Asian nations after the collapse of the totalitarian ideology of communism; these countries remain undemocratic. This is also true when totalitarian regimes collapse. Romania, Iran and Iraq are some examples of the struggles that ensue when totalitarian regimes fall and elections are held. The Bush administration's policies are against such recidivism in Iraq. Part of the twofold mission, regime change, has been accomplished, but the desire for the implementation of democracy has not come to fruition.

The question now is how will America ensure that only one of three possible outcomes prevails? Will the community adhere to democracy, Shiite dominated Islamic representative government, or a constant state of internal turmoil and fear brought about through terrorists and the ideology of Al Qaeda? The administration must empower Iraq's Shiites, Kurds and Sunnis looking to participate in government. The Shiites must take the dominant role because of their sheer numbers; this must occur in order for Iraqi citizens to overcome the brutality and fear of the terrorist organizations seeking to impose religious totalitarianism. Fear is clearly the post-Saddam approach that terrorists are seeking to create, and ominous clouds forecast more of the same for the near future. The Shiites have been delivered from a totalitarian regime through American occupation and are seeking political muscle. Fear-based models of government no longer imprison them. American occupation is viewed as a means to delivering a new foundation in Iraq.

But what is the foundation of such hope? Foundations are another issue to explore altogether. Some nations are based on religious beliefs and motivations, and other nations are based on secular, man-centered approaches to governing, but all seek to remain as autonomous as possible. The Western world progressed in spite of Absolutism, totalitarian regimes, and religious intolerance through a series of historical awakenings. Three movements shook the foundations of pre-existing philosophies and ushered in dramatic change for the West: the Renaissance, Reformation and Enlightenment took centuries to unfold. They were the frontrunners that gave rise to more liberal ideas and scientific rationale as a means of societal progress and tolerance in the pool of ideas. The previous ideas formed the foundational structure of modern democracy and democratic states. Much of Central Asia and the Middle East have no such history or foundation. Islam is the stated foundation of most statesmen in the region. These statesmen adhere to Sunnism or Shiism, and Shiism is dominant in Iraq and their immediate neighbor Iran as well. Iran is wary of US occupation, and Iraq's Shiites accept it for now, but this difference does not deeply divide the two countries.

The ties between the two Shia communities in Iraq and Iran give rise to the likely emergence of political Shiism as an influence in the region and a counter weight to democracy. Iran remains an enemy of the US and a sponsor of terrorism, yet decidedly Shiite. And Shiism is far more compatible within the overall culture than the foreign political ideology of democracy. There is a definite threat of a politically driven Shia emergence in the Middle East with anti-American sentiment. The implications are nothing less than a two-nation partnership working against US interest. America is assisting the nation of Iraq in numerous ways, but a stronger Iraq will look for other partners as well, and the most likely ally in this region will be Iran. Iran's influence in the region is increasing. It is flexing its muscles in the region due to the fact its ally, Russia, is assisting it with its nuclear capabilities. Iranian prospects of continued economic growth look promising as well. This Shiite nation is declaring the right to develop its own nuclear capabilities and to continue as a self-sustaining Islamic republic without interference or condemnation from the West.[2] It is also the most influential center in the Shia world. Iran recently boasted of its preparation to deal with the Western aggression through the use of suicide tactics. Below is an advertisement from State sponsored Iranian TV.

> **Commander Khamani has announced that registration for the suicide bomber force is open all over the country, and encourages Iranians to join in order to safeguard Islam and fight against its enemies. "This holy organization of the Islamic Republic is aimed at those who are interested in suicide. The volunteer will join specialist courses. Brothers and sisters who believe and are interested in defending Islam are invited to get in touch via P.O. Box Number 1653–664, Teheran, and are asked to send two photos, a copy of their birth certificate. Please enlist in the suicide squad.** (Taken from the Arab Television Network Al-Arabiya in July, 2005. Obtained and translated by MEMRI @ http://www.memri.org/)

Self-determination and self-reliance is a continuation of the policies of the Revolution of 1979, although the rhetoric is more subdued. The emergence of Shiism in the Iranian Revolution heightened the already existing division within the Sunni and Shiite communities. Shiites and Sunnis have divisions that have lasted since the death of Ali, the fourth Caliph. How will the growing Shia revival and the expression of Shiism impact the Middle East balance of power and threats? When Iraq chooses its direction it must answer the question of what is palatable for the population? [3] Self-determination is high on the list of Kurds, Sunnis and Shiites in Iraq.

The Shiites are emerging from the shadow of a fear-based approach towards them. Fear can be a motivational force that propels or stifles. Ideally, those who become experts in this predatory practice can immobilize their victim with the venom of threats and rapidly advance in such regimes, as a spider sprinting towards its trapped prey. Fear then becomes a societal norm, and leaders are chosen based on their skillful use of this tool. Fear will drive, stifle and most importantly ensure that the leadership remains in place. Will the Iraqis receive a fear-based model of leadership or alternative hope based models? It's safe to say that the fear-based model is something the terrorist networks want to continue. Two other options remain: democracy and political Shiism. The hope offered in democracy is second to the hope of Shiites who have the opportunity to become a truly powerful political force. This trumps any augmented hope the Bush administration has for Iraq. The Shiites amongst themselves need to form ties to offset the dominating influence of Sunnism in Islam.

Sunni and Shia politics, division and theology

Political divisions between Sunnis and Shiites are evident throughout the region. Shia emergence is not a small matter due to the fact many terrorists who claim Sunni allegiance will continue to react violently against Shiite empowerment and the occupation, while Sunnis will, at the very least, resent the appearance of Shiite political legitimacy. Shiite emergence in the Middle East will also prove to be a political stumbling block that ignites religious animosity and political struggle between the two major branches of professing Muslims. It is no stretch to state that a large number of Sunnis regard Shiites as secondary believers, a smaller number consider them infidels. This is one of the reasons Shiites have been oppressed in several nations, even though they have a larger numerical presence in some of these countries.[4] The vested hopes of American democracy in the Middle East will stand or fall based on the outcome of Iraq. If the Bush administration takes a long hard look at Shiism, they will recognize the hold the faith has over the people, and they will not attempt to undermine the imams, considered infallible by Shiites. They will seek to engage them, and bring them into the political process, and offer incentives for progressive theology, even if it means their idea of democracy will not be achieved. Progressive Shia Islam with democratic principles should be the goal. A cursory look at Shiism will give insight into its followers now present in occupied Iraq.

Shia theology is repugnant to a great number of Sunnis who believe that the Shiites fabricated some Hadiths. (Sayings of the Prophets, as documented by faithful followers and companions, these books are secondary to the Quran but serve as buttresses for Islamic law and way of life.) The charges of fabrication toward the Shiites and illegitimate possession of the Caliphate toward the Sunnis, are not small accusations in the Islamic Ummah. The question that arises is simply one of credibility. Right and wrong must be answered by the true believers, lest they stray from the path of righteousness; to date, this divide has not been mended.[5] The lack of regard for Shiite traditions has been highlighted by the condemnation of several Sunni clerics who have condemned the marches of Shiites to holy shrines; the clerics believe the partisans of Ali are actively practicing idolatry by participating in these rituals.[6] Terrorist organizations welcome such statements and are emboldened by them. Attacks on the Shiites are becoming more frequent and commonplace and are justified by the theological babblings of terrorist organizations. The continued struggle for legitimate identity within Islam has endured, and Shiites continue to ardently hold to their beliefs, tighter than a poor man's fist clinging to his last dollar.

The acute power struggle and desire for the recognition of stewardship of the true faith has continued to rage for some time. The math is clear; Shiites represent anywhere from 12 to 15% of the total number of people who claim allegiance to Allah. The number of Muslims in the world adds up to roughly 1.25 billion. This gives us a range of 146 million to 195 million Shiites who live between the geographical area of Lebanon and Pakistan. The ideological centers of power in the Islamic world emanate from the Shiite faith in Tehran (and some centers in Iraq) and the Sunnis in Mecca, the origin of the faith. Saudi Arabia actively supported a policy of containing Shia influence by inculcating Sunni populations with anti-Shia sentiment and exporting Wahhabism abroad. It was a matter of policy for Riyadh to bolster anti-Shia sentiment because of the emergence of Iran as the only Shiite regional power in the Islamic world. This took place after the return and rise of Ayatollah Khomeini during the Islamic Revolution of Iran.[7] This revolution sparked a strong Sunni response, captured best by Saudi Arabia.

Spreading Wahhabism, rigid puritanical version of Islam that is also the state religion, was a matter of foreign policy for Saudi Arabia. They recognized the need to have a two-fold approach toward Russian aggression in Afghanistan and Shiite emergence via Iran in the region. Wahhabism began to flourish during this period as clerics and the royal family pressed this objective into Pakistan and abroad. This served as a barrier to Iran's influence and served Pakistan's interest in Kashmir. Madrassahs were constructed and funded, and they were instructed to create a worldview in the minds of the students that espoused the virtues of Islam and militant jihad in some centers. This in turn created zeal in the converts who in turn sought to purge the faith from heresy and hypocrisy. Saudi Arabia's continued policy toward Iran, and the Shia movement paid off when the US, and virtually all of the Sunni governments supported Iraq in the Iraq/Iran War.[8] This setback for the only powerful Shiite nation was devastating, but they continued to persevere in light of their proud history and the prophetic certainty of their future. The vessels of such light would be the imams and the inevitable rise of another Caliphate.

The issue of a true caliphate, divinely guided leader that all Muslims should follow, took center stage after the death of Muhammad. The Ummah, community of believers, needed to be unified, because there was no clear successor to Muhammad. The caliphate fell, by election, on Abu Bakr then Umar, Uthman and finally Ali. The Shia hold that the first three Caliphs were not legitimate and that Ali, the cousin and son in law of Muhammad, should have succeeded Muhammad. The Shia, partisans of Ali, split from the larger body. Later they split into three groups: Zaydis, Ismailis and the Ithnas or Twelvers. Although there are disparate groups within the Shia, all venerate the imam as the highest authority in the Ummah who is divinely appointed. Due to the fact that the imam is elevated to such a high level, it would explain some of the control and sway that the imam has held over Shiites. The doctrine and person of the Mahdi cannot be discarded either. The role of an emerging Mahdi is nothing short of miraculous, and this doctrine builds from several other foundations established within Shia Islam that are distinct from Sunnism.

These doctrines established some of the major differences and progressive thought of Shiite theology. The distinctions are evident, but less visible are the historical facts concerning persecution. Shiites have been persecuted throughout the generations of their pilgrimage in Islam. Themes of suffering, oppression and hope have become very prevalent, one could even say expected. With this in mind the role the imam becomes more important.[9] Below are lists of doctrinal approaches of Shiites and the original preeminent imams that the predominate number of Shiites (Twelvers) esteem. The lists of imam's is important because there were 12, each appointed by his successor in an unbroken chain. They also possessed *walayat* or spiritual guidance that kept them free from error and sin. The imams are all descended from Ali, and they form the cornerstone of Shiism.

- The *Shi'a* call to prayer and declaration of faith reflect its glorification of the Caliph Ali;

- *Shi'ahs* revere "the five holy ones" as the Prophet Muhammad, his daughter Fátima al-Zahra, the Prophet's son-in-law Alí, and the Prophet's grandchildren Hasan and Husayn;

- *Shi'ahs* may recognize different "hadith" or prophetic traditions, favoring those offered by Ali and his wife, Fatima, to those of Aishah, the Prophet's youngest wife, who opposed Ali;

- *Shi'a Islam* accepts four authentic "Books of Tradition" of the Hadiths;

- The *Shi'a* venerate the fourteen "rightly guided" leaders as the Prophet Muhammad, Fátima al-Zahra, and the Twelve Imams, described below;

- *Shi'a* hold as sacred the martyrdom of Ali and Husayn;

- *Shi'a* Muslims believe in the *Mahdi*, similar to the coming of a messiah [10]

List of 12 Imams
The First Imam
Amirul Momineen Ali

Father: Abu Talib bin Abdul Muttalib bin Hashim.

Mother: Fatimah bint Asad bin Hashim bin Abd Munaf.

Kunniyat (Patronymic): Abul Hasan and Husayn, Abu Turab

Laqab (Title): Al-Wasi, Amir al-Mu'minin

Birth: He was born in the Ka'ba, in thirty 'Am al-Fil (the year of the elephant).

Martyrdom: He was martyred by the Khwariji named Abd al-Rahman ibn Muljam at Kufa during the month of Ramadhan in the fortieth year of Hijrah and is buried in Najaf on the outskirts of Kufa.

The Second Imam
Al-Hasan ibn Ali ibn Abi Talib

Mother: Fatimah az-Zahra (a.s.), the daughter of the Holy Prophet (s.a.w.s.).

Kunniyat (Patronymic): Abu Muhammad

Laqab (Title): Al-Sibt al-Kabir (the elder grandson), Al-Mujtaba.

Birth: He was born in Madina in the middle of the month of Ramadhan in 3 A.H.

Martyrdom: He died on the 28th of Safar in the year 50 A.H. He was buried in the graveyard of Baqi in Madina.

The Third Imam
Al-Husayn ibn Ali ibn Abi Talib

Mother: Fatimah az-Zahra (a.s.), the daughter of the Holy Prophet (s.a.w.s.).

Kunniyat (Patronymic): Abu 'Abdillah.

Laqab (Title): Al Sibt, Shahid-e-Karbala.

Birth: He was born in Madina in the month of Shaban in the year 4 A.H.

Martyrdom: He was martyred with his companions by the army of Yazid in the month of Muharram 61 A.H. His tomb is in Karbala, a town of Iraq.

The Fourth Imam
Ali ibn Al-Husayn (a.s.)

Mother: Ghazala, Shahzanaan

Kunniyat (Patronymic): Abu al-Hasan

Laqab (Title): Zayn al-'Abidin, Al Sajjad

Birth: He was born in 38 A.H. in Madina.

Martyrdom: He died of poison in the year 94 or 95 A.H. at Madina and is buried at Baqi near his uncle Hasan (a.s.).

The Fifth Imam
Muhammad ibn Ali

Mother: Umm Abdullah, the daughter of Imam Hasan (a.s.).

Kunniyat (Patronymic): Abu Ja'far.

Laqab (Title): Al Baqir.

Birth: He was born at Madina in the year 57 A.H.

Martyrdom: He died of poisoning in Madina in 114 A.H. and is also buried at Baqi near his father.

The Sixth Imam
Ja'far ibn Muhammad (a.s.)

Mother: Umm Farwa, the daughter of Qasim bin Muhammad bin Abu Bakr.

Kunniyat (Patronymic): Abu 'Abdillah.

Laqab (Title): Al-Sadiq.

Birth: He was born at Madina in 83 A.H.

Martyrdom: He died of poison in 148 A.H. and is buried at Baqi near his father.

The Seventh Imam
Musa bin Ja'far

Mother: Hamidah

Kunniyat (Patronymic): Abu al-Hasan

Laqab (Title): Al-Kazim

Birth: He was born at Madina in the year 129 A.H.

Martyrdom: He was poisoned in the prison of Harun al-Rashid at Baghdad in the year 183 A.H. He is buried in Kazimiyyah in Iraq.

The Eighth Imam
Ali bin Musa

Mother: Al Khayzran

Kunniyat (Patronymic): Abu al-Hasan

Laqab (Title): Al-Rida

Birth: He was born at Madina in 148 A.H.

Martyrdom: He was poisoned in the year 203 A.H. and is buried in the Khurasan district of Iran.

The Ninth Imam
Muhammad bin Ali

Mother: Sakina

Kunniyat (Patronymic): Abu 'Abdillah

Laqab (Title): Al Jawad

Birth: He was born at Madina in 195 A.H.

Martyrdom: He died of poison at Baghdad in the year 220 A.H. and is buried near his grandfather at Kazimiyyah in Iraq.

The Tenth Imam
Ali bin Muhammad

Mother: Samana al-Maghribiya

Kunniyat (Patronymic): Abu al-Hasan al Askari

Laqab (Title): Al Hadi

Birth: He was born at Madina in the year 212 A.H.

Martyrdom: He died of poison in 254 A.H. at Samarrah (Sarmanra) in Iraq and is buried there.

The Eleventh Imam
Al Hasan bin Ali

Mother: Ummul Walad—Susan.

Kunniyat (Patronymic): Abu Muhammad.

Laqab (Title): Al Askari.

Birth: He was born at Samarrah in the year 232 A.H.

Martyrdom: He was poisoned in 260 A.H. at Samarrah and is buried there.

All the tombs of the eleven Imams (a.s.) are a place of Ziyarat (visitation) by Muslims. Four of the Imams are buried at Baqi in Madina al-Munawwara. However, their tombs were demolished by the authorities along with the tombs of the wives of the Prophet (s.a.w.s.) and his companions.

The Twelfth Imam
Al Hujjat Muhammad ibn al-Hasan

Mother: Ummul Walad Narjis alias Saiqal

Kunniyat (Patronymic): Abu 'Abdullah, Abu al-Qasim

Laqab (Title): Al-Qaim, Al-Muntazar, Al-Khalaf, Al-Mahdi, Sahib al-zamaan.

Birth: He was born at Samarrah in the year 255 A.H. He is the last Imam (a.s.) and he is alive and hidden.[11]

Guidance and deliverance are prevalent themes today in Shiism. The imams, corporately armed with *walayat* to guide them, have a receptive audience. The Shiites have endured a great deal in Iraq recently. Previous hardships and the viscous of faith in their Imams have caused Shiites to use great restraint in dealing with terrorists. With these things in mind, we must look at the response of Shiites when faced with the consistent onslaught of bombings in Iraq; remarkable restraint remains. The aims of the terrorists' insurgency are ultimately to keep a Shiite dominated country from maintaining power as evidenced in the chronology of bombings. Occupation by the hands of a foreign government is one thing, but the reality is this; many of the bombings target other Iraqis who are often Shiites. Many Shiites are participating in the newly formed government and are thereby targets of the militants who claim Sunni affiliation and are Al Qaeda operatives or follow their doctrines. The litany of bombings also requires careful attention, because the aims of those participating in these attacks are clear; they seek to inflict as much damage and chaos as possible. The Al Qaeda affiliated Zarqawi network and others are fighting against incredible odds, persisting due to the fact they believe in their cause and are motivated by a deep hatred of Western influence, occupation and the Shiite emergence in Iraq. In their view, Islam, their version, is under attack from the crusaders and those who follow a perverse form of the faith, namely the Shiites. The death toll for Shiites in Iraq that have fallen due to the terrorist attacks is roughly estimated to be 11,000–12,000. [12]

Deliverers and Liberators

American democracy, Shiism and Terrorists have claimed the title of deliverers or liberators. The politics of oppression is at work and a central thought in need of addressing. People respond to the idea that there are oppressive forces at work that can only be removed by bloodshed. The forces of oppression take root primarily in the form of an aggressive nation or a nation that oppresses its population. [13] The primary aim of any movement that purportedly speaks for the downtrodden is to win the hearts and minds of the people. Taxing are the sacrifices that America, Shiites and terrorist networks demand of their followers. At the end of the day, there is a tremendous amount of pressure exerted to win the devotion to the cause. Shiites and terrorists are fighting to usher in righteousness and the preeminent days of their version of Islam. They believe a righteous caliph who is the guardian of a state can achieve this. Al Qaeda's ideas have converted many who are not active members and its affiliates attempt to speak to discontent Sunnis, gathering their criminal/soldier organization to Iraq in order to play deliverer. But this is a role America has reserved for itself. Deliverance of the land from apostate rulers and occupiers is a constant theme in Al Qaeda's doctrine and Al Qaeda is giving privileged youth like the 9/11 hijackers the opportunity to embark on deliverance. Al Qaeda and adherents to its doctrines seek a revolution in all Islamic countries in order to ensure their version of Islam rules over nations. The desire for statehood and a home for a righteous caliphate rest squarely on the shoulders of the youth within the Ummah. Oppressed people look for a liberator, from within their borders, outside, or from the heavens. The majority of Islamic populations fall into the category of oppressed. When there are themes of oppression and occupation, there is a hope for deliverers. Militant cults capitalize on this yearning, and suicide operations have increase.

My conclusions on global emergence of suicide operations: Militant cults and pragmatism or nationalism?

As I have argued in my earlier papers that deal with militant cults, there is no remittance that can compete with an idea. This has been proven time and time again. The preeminent suicide operatives that have struck the West were not poor, uneducated or oppressed. They did not commit these acts in order to have money for their families; they were deliverers. They believed that they were doing something on the behalf of those who could not act on their own behalf and for their God. The extreme self-deception Al Qaeda ideology espouses is taking root in Iraq and beyond just as it has in other places, and other militant cults sell a similar idea. Other groups sell and proselytize based on an idea. Whether a city in this life, one beyond it, or one's name living beyond his death, the issue here is what I call martyrdom seeds. Oppressed people and their self proclaimed deliverers face overwhelming odds when trying to accomplish their purposes, and some are willing to lose their lives as martyrs in hopes that their seed will live on in one form or another. The trice is the *promise of an afterlife and significance beyond the grave*, whether secular or otherwise. We have to look at the promise as an inducement. As a proponent of my militant cult theory I must address the findings of a provocative and well-researched book recently published that attacks the significance of ideas or religion in suicide operations. The book is Dr. Robert Pape's, *Dying to Win. It is a statistically packed book that takes another look at terrorism. He uses the lens of nationalism to explain the phenomena of suicide operations and proceeds to prescribe a strategy for Iraq. In short, leave and return to offshore bal-*

ancing. He puts forth a theory based on statistical data and his interpretation of the data leads him to conclude that suicide terrorism is the result of three things:

1. **National resistance to an occupying power**

2. **The occupying power is democratic**

3. **There is a difference of religion between the occupier and the occupied.** [14]

According to his findings religion plays a secondary role behind nationalism. He states that the occupier's religion is more important than the one who is occupied. I agree with some of his findings, namely the importance of land to people and how secular groups can employ suicide operations effectively, but his lack of belief in the power of nonmaterial ideas and their viscous is disturbing and shows his lack of experience in faith or idea based beliefs. The religious scholars and philosophy scholars understand this, but he clearly is dismissive. His over reliance on the data collected from regional jihads and the Tamil Tigers skews the entire study and does not convincingly address other acts of terrorism carried out by supranationalist organizations such as the Al Qaeda network, or their desire to acquire greater weapons for the sake of a continued global campaign. He also ignores what many devout Muslims who have seen this at work in their communities are saying about suicide terrorism. His answer is to leave the region in order to prevent suicide operations. [15]

There is a utilitarian purpose behind suicide bombings that all agree on; this is not a revelation or something his research has brought to the surface. His research is valuable and places suicide bombings within the realm of rational actors and for that his contributions are to be commended. However, Before September 11th the prevailing notions were that suicide operations were local and act only out of desperation. Pape would have us believe that these are still the primary causes. I could not differ more. I have some contentions with his theory, primarily the following, because his conclusions are refurbished ideas focused on regional struggles that predate Al Qaeda's emergence, and fail to address the supranational spread of the virus of militant cults.

    1.   Dr. Pape fails to adequately address the supranational dimension of Al Qaeda and dismisses the power of religious motivation altogether, except for the occupier's religion. He states that the religious beliefs of most of Hezbollah's suicide bombers were secular or Christian. The counterpoint is this, regardless of his conclusions concerning the bombers, they were acting as members of a radical militant cult that was more than willing to

exploit them. He over relies on the data of the Tamil Tigers because they are secular, but he fails to address the fact that religion is a cultural, regional and national phenomenon. The leader of the Tamil tiger's created a belief system, partially borrowed from Marxism and infused with myths, that would foster such actions, and it could arguably be called a religion because of the heavy reliance on symbolism and sacrifice. When coupled with the cult-like devotion of the followers one could call this a militant cult that believed the only way to be significant beyond the grave is to achieve martyrdom. [16] Marxist beliefs are every bit as stringent as a religion, because the Marxist believes in the *inevitable* conquest of Marxism's enemies. This belief in fate and inevitability encourages believers in this idea to surrender to fate.

2. Dr. Pape fails to sufficiently address the issue of exported suicide operations and the fact that young people born in their home countries are acting on the behalf of Al Qaeda, other terrorist organizations or an idea used to inspire acts of violence.

3. One grievous oversight in his book is the lack of attention given to the fact that terrorists regularly target members of their religious communities, even children. They justify this by demonizing them with the name of apostate and carry out their actions.

4. Dr. Pape declares there is a reason no suicide bombings in Iraq were present before, the absence of occupation. [17] It is obvious that when one possesses superior weapons there is no need to resort to those tactics. The Al Mahdi militia fought but did not use these tactics against the US occupation. He also leaves out the fact that Iraq's regime ruled with an iron fist, never allowing citizens to arm themselves. Suicide operations are an effective tactic, but not always a last resort. They are sometimes used to show people the level of commitment their group possesses. Pape leaves out the fact that Al Qaeda's leader in Iraq, Al Zarqawi, is a foreigner, with no purpose other than destruction. He is also actively targeting members of his Sunni faith and Shiites, who do not need his deliverance. In short, Pape's explanation falls short.

In conclusion, there are many voices currently sounding off on Iraq, and a great deal are making statements that simply cannot account for a sound approach to the imminent problems America faces in this region. I offer the following prescriptions for dealing with Iraq and the three supranational ideas.

1. Ensure that the populace deems free elections legitimate.

2. Emphasize independence from Iran and the quietist approach of Al Sistanti's view of the imam's political involvement, which is different than Iran's Ayatollahs.

3. Continue to engage the Shiites, Sunnis and Kurds, and focus on the reality that there will be a more powerful Shia political reality that we helped to create. Emphasize the Arab commonality they have with other Middle Eastern nations America has developed ties with. Point out the isolationist politics that Iran practices in the Middle East. Reward participation with the promise of continued financial and military support for insurgencies and terrorist activity.

4. Continue to raise concerns about Iran's support of terrorist orgs and nuclear ambitions. Push for sanctions because of the nuclear issue.

5. Make clear distinctions between terrorist movements and insurgencies; they are not the same and insurgencies can sometimes be solved through diplomatic means. The Al Sadr Mahdi militia negotiation was an example of success.

6. Treat the religious leaders, imams, and mosques in Iraq as powerful centers of influence due to the sway they have over the citizens. Al Sistani is one example of an imam holding tremendous sway. He has kept the Shiites from responding violently towards the Sunnis in Iraq.

7. Encourage mutual fatwas by Sunnis and Shiites that clarify what acts are permitted during jihad, and encourage them to further ostracize the terrorists.

8. Train Iraqis to provide security for the premier clerics in Iraq, because no political process will be deemed legitimate if the clerics are against it or fall victim to assassination. This is not appeasement of the clerics; it is simply the reality of the culture.

9. Make sure the minority populations and religions are treated more equitably when any constitution that is finalized

10. Make future benefits and aid dependent upon reaching rubrics of any democratic process

Some of the above are taking place in Iraq, but democratic idealism cannot permeate the entire process. America must accept the fact that it can effectively deal with a progressive Shia polity and attempt to move the process for greater democracy forward. If America pushes too hard, too fast we will drive the newly formed government into a greater partnership with Iran, and that is something

America is unwilling to deal with. In short, Iraq has previously been within the grip of tyrannical oppression, but it is now occupied, and rapidly changing with three deliverers at hand. Three ideas remain:

1. Al Qaeda's expanding ideology and influence that is giving birth to a murderous rampage, insurgency and later…perhaps civil war.

2. Bush continues to push democratic idealism, but it must be modified to be effective.

3. The emergence of Shiism as a political/religious force that is ultimately awaiting Al Mahdi, the Rightly Guided One. This is the likely outcome.

Shiism as a political force will emerge from this and America will be the instrument of this unleashing.

1 Bush has made this statement repeatedly in public speeches dating back to the axis of evil comments at the State of the Union Address, January 30, 2002
3 William O. Beema, George W. Bush—The 13th Shi'a Imam, Accessed, http://www.truthout.org/cgi-bin/artman/exec/view.cgi/38/9473 t r u t h o u t | Perspective Monday 07 March 2005, accessed 7/10/2005 3:00 PM
4. By Michael S. Doran, Intimate Enemies,Wednesday, February 18, 2004; Page A19
5 William Obeema, George W. Bush—The 13th Shia Imam
6 Nasr, Vali "Regional Implications of Shia Revival in Iraq" The Center For Strategic and International Studies and The Massachusetts Institute of Technology, *The Washington Quarterly*, 27.3 pp.7–24, 2004 Accessed on 7/11/05, 6:30 PM http://www.twq.com/04summer/docs/04summer_nasr.pdf
7 Ibid.
8 Ibid
9 Herald (Karachi), September 92, p. 34
10 Alliance for Security, "What Do We Know About Shiism?" http://www.allianceforsecurity.org/shiah accessed at 1:19 PM, July, 17, 2005 PM
11 Ibid.
12 Knickmeyer, Ellen, The Washington Post Foreign Service, June,3 2005, Accessed at Washington Post.com, http://www.washingtonpost.com/wp-dyn/content/article/2005/06/02/AR2005060201098.html, 7/9/2005
13 Sayyid Murtada al-'Askari, ***The Twelve Successors of the Holy Prophet (peace be upon him and his Progeny)*Translation by:** Al-Qalam Translators and Writers Bureau,[Some corrections and content enrichment by the Ahlul Bayt DILP team], *Published by:*World Islamic Network (WIN), 67/69 H. Abbas (a.s.) Street, Dongri,
Mumbai—400 009. India, http://www.al-islam.org/twelve/ accessed on 7/24/05, 6:00 PM
14 Pape, Robert, *Dying to Win: The Strategic Logic of Suicide Bombing*, May, 2005 (Random House Publishing Inc, New York), pp.126,27
15 Pape, pp. 246-247
16 Carey, Benedict, "Method Without Madness," Los Angeles Times, July 30, 2002
17 Pape, 246

Comments and Reflections On North Korea: The Darkness Remains

Fall 2005

North Korea is a place where myth and illusion under the guise of self reliance are used as the impetuses for securing the death of individualism. The people are perpetually indoctrinated into servile obedience to the Cult of the Kim Dynasty. Starvations, imprisonment, state sanctioned atrocities and a general disregard for human life are the norm in this place. If the Devil chose a vacation spot on earth, he would find North Korea a suitable place due to the skillful use of deception, cruelty and brain washing as a means of gaining devotion.

The author

The most alarming feature of North Korea is the stream of stark tales of terror consistently told by those who were fortunate enough to escape. Although named in President Bush's Axis of evil in the fall of 2001, few Americans know just how perverse and dark this country's leadership is; neither are the majority of Americans aware of the character traits of Kim Jung Il, the ruthless dictator who governs the nation. His father created the false foundation of self reliance called juche and he continues the illusion. It propels the population to unquestionably serve the whims of Kim Jung Il. This is a form of self reliance that teaches man is the master of his destiny. North Korea's national identity rest on the myths propagated by the Kim Dynasty's claim that the father (although dead is considered the eternal president) and son are the embodiment of juche. North Koreans are told to persevere until the coming of promised revolution that will unify Korea once again.

Therefore, juche is seen as both a personal struggle and a national struggle fused into a movement of liberation. [1] With this in mind one must ask the question of what type of liberation the people are striving for and what earthly paradise does the Cult of Kim Jung Il offer. The answer is the illusion of an emerging Korean utopia. The reality is much worse for the common North Korean and even worse for those who do not measure up to the ideal of juche. It is a vile place for all and worse for those who attempt to make it better. Any deviance or incompetence is met by imprisonment of offender and family. Imprisonment is preferred because of the slave labor it produces. The following pages are taken from the highest ranking North Korean government defector.

These comments and quotes were delivered in front United States Committee on the Judiciary, June 21st 2002, Testimony of Ms. Soon

Ok Lee North Korean prison camp survivor Seoul, South Korea. (No statements are altered from the original statements.)

I was a normal gullible North Korean citizen, loyal to Leader and Party, and believed that North Korea was a people's paradise. I was the Director of the Government Supply Office for party cadres for 14 years when I was arrested in 1984 under the false charge of embezzlement of state property. I was subjected to severe torture during a 14 month preliminary investigation until I was forced to admit to the false charges against her. Eventually, I received a term of 13 years in prison at a kangaroo court. I had served 5 years and two months in prison when I was released in 1992 under a surprise amnesty.

I recollect life in the North Korean prison:

"A prisoner has no right to talk, laugh, sing or look in a mirror. Prisoners must kneel down on the ground and keep their heads down deeply whenever called by a guard, they can say nothing except to answer questions asked. Women prisoners' babies are killed on delivery. Prisoners have to work as slaves for 18 hours daily. Repeated failure to meet the work quotas means a week's time in a punishment cell. A prisoner must give up her human worth. When I was released, some 6,000 prisoners, both men and women, were crying and pleading with me in their hearts to let the outside world know of their suffering. How can I ever forget their eyes, the eyes of the tailless beasts?"

Meals for Prisoners

Salt soup
100 grams of broken corn, full meal
80 grams of broken corn, reduced for punishment
60 grams of broken corn, reduced for punishment
Prisoners' Sleeping Conditions
Some eighty to ninety prisoners sleep in a flea infested chamber about six meters long by five meters wide (about 19 feet by 16 feet). Some eighty percent of the prisoners are housewives. The prison chamber is so congested that sleeping there is itself a torture. Prisoners sleep on the floor, squeezed together, head and feet alternating. So, prisoners sleep with the stinking feet of other prisoners right under their nose. They roll up their clothes for pillows.
During the winter, prisoners share body heat against the cold wind coming under the floor. However, during the summer, it is so stuffy with the sweat and stink of the prisoners that they prefer sleeping at the work site even though it means more work. Two prisoners must stand on night duty for one hour shifts. The following morning, prisoners on night duty must report to the prison authorities all the details of their duty including the sleep talking of other prisoners. They get their duty hour extended if caught sleeping.

Prisoners and Prison Guards

At all the factories, there are glass boxes for prison guards to sit in while supervising prisoners at work. The glass walls enable them to watch the prisoners at work while avoiding their terrible stench. In addition, the prison guards always wear masks and keep some distance from the prisoners because of the bad smell.

As standard practice, a prisoner must run to the official and sit down on her knees with her head down whenever she is called. The prisoner can only answer the questions asked and cannot say anything else. Prisoners are very often kicked in the face or breast for slow answers or movement. The prisoners are severely punished for raising their heads or stretching their bodies.

Punishment Cells, Chambers of Death

The punishment cell is one of the most dreaded punishments for all prisoners. The cells are usually 60 cm wide and 110 cm high. Therefore, the prisoners have no room to stand up, stretch their legs or lie down. They cannot even lean against the walls because they are too jagged. There are twenty such cells for female prisoners and 58 cells for male prisoners. They are usually detained for seven to ten days as punishment for certain offenses, such as leaving an oily mark on clothes, failing to memorize the president's New Year message or repeated failure to meet work quotas.

When the prisoners are released from the cells, their legs are badly bent, with frostbite in the winter, and so they can hardly walk. Many victims are permanently crippled from the lack of adequate exercise and eventually died as a result of the work resumed immediately after the release. The prisoners call the punishment cell *"Chilsong Chamber," meaning a black angel's chamber of death.*

In November 1989, I was detained in the punishment cell for a week for attempting to cover up a faulty piece of shirt made by a 20 year old girl. The young girl was sent to the torture chamber and never seen again. Among other things, the freezing cold wind from the toilet hole made the experience extremely painful. During the summer, the prisoners struggle to brush thousands of maggots back into the toilet hole.

After being released, I had problems walking for 15 days, but I was able to recover because my job gave me the needed opportunity to walk to all corners of the prison with work instructions. They say it is a day of great fortune if a prisoner finds a rat creeping up from the bottom of the toilet hole. The prisoners catch it with their bare hands and devour it raw, as rats are the only source of meat in the prison. They say the wonderful taste of a raw rat is unforgettable. If they are caught eating a rat, however, the punishment is extended. So they have to be very careful when catching and eating a rat.

Prisoners Die After Spending Time in Punishment Cell

Hun sik Kim was the principal of Pyongyang Light Engineering College. She was sentenced to a 5 year imprisonment for suggesting to the City Education

Board that her students' labor responsibility be reduced so that they could spend more time studying.

In prison, she was assigned the work of measuring fabric to produce jackets, which were to be given as gifts to workers outside by the President on his birthday. One time, she miscalculated the imported nylon fabric but immediately corrected the error and no fabric was wasted. However, she was detained in the punishment cell for ten days for "attempting sabotage." She was crippled and partly paralyzed when she was released from the punishment cell. On a very hot summer day in August, the camp doctors burned her bottom with heated stones to see if she could feel pain. Just before she died a few weeks later, she whispered to me, with a twittered tongue and tears in her eyes, "I want to see the blue sky. You know my children are waiting for me."

When she was released from the punishment cell, she needed two prisoners to help her walk to the work site and back. The camp officials claimed that she was feigning injury, and yelled, "You bitch! Who do you think you are fooling?"

She was kicked around like a soccer ball by the guards but withstood the insults and beatings for about a month. She suffered injuries all over her body while pulling herself up. The sores began to badly suppurate from the infections. She often fainted. She was sent to the sick room but she had to continue her work in the sick room. I was in the same room because I was a paratyphoid patient. One day in August, the camp doctors burned her with heated stones to see if she could feel pain. I could smell flesh burning, and felt like vomiting and fainting. I remembered what the camp official told me when I first arrived at the camp, "You must give up all your rights as a human!" She never felt any pain when her flesh was burning.

From that day on, she could not control urination and evacuation. I was suffering from a high fever myself but tried my best to caress her burnt wounds with the dirty cloth the doctors gave me. "I want to see the blue sky. You know my children are waiting for me."

The next few days, I felt very sick and was unconscious myself, so nobody looked after her as she kept moaning. A few days later, I came to myself, crawled to her and removed the cloth from her wound. I was shocked to see the wound full of maggots! She died that night. I shouted to a guard through the small door hole, "Sir, somebody died here." The reply was, "So what? You bitch! Don't panic. Wait until morning!" I found the floor full of maggots the following morning. I had to brush the floor with my bare hands and pick up the maggots into a vinyl bag. I told myself, "You must not die like this. You must survive and tell the whole world about it."

Prisoners Beaten Cruelly

One common form of torture was to tie a prisoner against iron bars, spread eagle by hands and legs and beat him all over the body with a rubber or cow skin whip. Just the pain from hanging by your body weight makes the ordeal unbearable. From the beatings, the skin becomes torn all over, blood splashes and the prisoners begin to feel that their skin isn't human any more. When a prisoner is released from the iron bar, his whole body is so swollen that he cannot bend his back or knees. The prisoner must evacuate and urinate standing. In the Nongpo Police Detention Center, there were three torture chambers and all kinds of torture were routinely practiced on inmates. I was 39 years old at that time. They subjected me to all kinds of torture there.

Once I resisted when they tried to undress me. One of the torturers punched me in my face so hard that I fainted to the floor. Sometime later, I woke up to find my mouth full of something. They were my broken teeth. Obviously, I bled terribly because the floor was full of my blood. My face was so badly swollen that I could hardly open my eyes. I spit out the broken teeth only after holding up my lips with my fingers. Four teeth from the upper jaw were gone. I began to feel terrible pain in my other teeth. Usually, I was taken to the torture chamber at five o'clock in the morning and remained there until midnight.

Tearing Off the Ears of a Prisoner

The Comptroller of the Seamen's Club of Chongjin City was an old man, 60 years old. He could no longer withstand the tortures that continued daily. When the investigators tore off one of his ears and began tearing off the other, he decided to please the investigators by claiming to be a big thief the bigger the better. So, he told them that he stole a locomotive from the city railway station. He acquired the nickname, "locomotive head" from the police investigators and officers.

Christians Killed for Refusing to Convert

The cast iron factory was considered the most difficult place to work in the entire prison. Christians were usually sent there to work. One Christian working at the cast iron factory was killed by hanging in a public execution in December 1988 for hiding a friend at his house before he was arrested.

In the spring of 1990, I was carrying a work order to the cast iron factory in the male prison. Five or six elderly Christians were lined up and forced to deny their Christianity and accept the Juche Ideology of the State. The selected prisoners all remained silent at the repeated command for conversion. The security officers became furious by this and killed them by pouring molten iron on them one by one.

The quotes from this account are repeated by numerous survivors of prison camps. This tells the author one thing, the Cult of Kim is by far the worse industrialized regime on the face of the earth. He completely controls the population through trices, threats and treachery. There is no justification for this cult like regime's continued existence except for other nations' fear of its nuclear capabilities and it ties to China and Russia. North Korea snubs its nose at the world with impunity and will one day be proven as a nation that sponsors terrorism, exports WMDs, while diverting economic aid for its citizens to the purpose of military buildup. The author's assessment of North Korea may seem extreme because it is true that nations do look at each other with great distrust and point out their enemy's hypocrisy. Reinhold Neibhur said it best. "Nations will always find it more difficult to find the beam that is in their own eye while they observe the mote in their brother's eye; and individuals find it difficult enough. A perennial weakness in the moral life of individuals is simply raised to the nth degree in national life." [2] But we ignore the mote in North Korea's eye to our own hurt.

1. Kim Il Sung, "Eradicating Dogmatism and Formalism by Consolidating Juche" (December 28, 1955).
2. Neibuhr, Reinhold, *The Nature and Destiny of Man,* 2 vols. (New York; Charles Scribners Sons, 1949) p. 107

Epilogue

This book was part of a journey I've taken. The pages are the result of a great deal of discussion, reading, and even more thinking. I've learned throughout this journey that agility of mind is necessary. One must have an interest in politics, theology, philosophy and the social sciences in order to remain relevant. But there are salient thoughts that remain in my mind, concerning the work. The dominant thought is that it has fallen short of what I would have liked to present to the public, but it is within the realm of satisfactory. Part of the reason it has fallen short is my personal biases, limits on time, no working foreign language skills, lack of actual visits to the countries mentioned, lack of sophisticated, statistical correlation to support my militant cult theory and the realism lenses through which I view the data. We all have constructs of philosophical barriers and worldviews that hinder our objectivity. We pride ourselves in stating we look only at the facts, but with human beings this is never the case. My philosophical construct can accurately be called Christian Realism. I'm am aware of the limits of any work that purports to instruct and examine terrorism or national security, but I am also aware of the fact that this present age is beset by conflict, war and bloodshed. There is no easy solution to the terror and cruelty that springs from fallen human nature. Ideas such as radical jihad are often the clothing of malevolent intent by selfish individuals. And governments often use their ideas as fig leaves to cover self interests. These things should be kept in mind as one continues his research. On this journey I am but one watchman who may have misinterpreted the data. Nevertheless I feel that I have alerted people to the dangers lying ahead for this country, and my fervent hope is that I am wrong and that I can relax and *chill,* but I don't believe that will be the case. I'll stand and watch the horizon and let you know what I see next.

978-0-595-37033-7
0-595-37033-0

www.ingramcontent.com/pod-product-compliance
Lightning Source LLC
Chambersburg PA
CBHW020422290526
45785CB00002B/689